Every Play Revealed
Volume I:
Oregon vs Ohio State

Alex Kirby

ISBN: 1517019051
ISBN-13: 978-1517019051

INTRODUCTION

This book is a breakdown of the first College Football Playoff National Championship Game.

It is organized in chronological order, starting with the opening kickoff, and ending with the final play. Each offensive/defensive play is diagrammed with a commentary below the picture, as well as a summary after the completion of each drive with thoughts on both teams.

Special teams plays have been diagrammed as well, with occasional analysis.

I hope you enjoy the book.

Alex Kirby

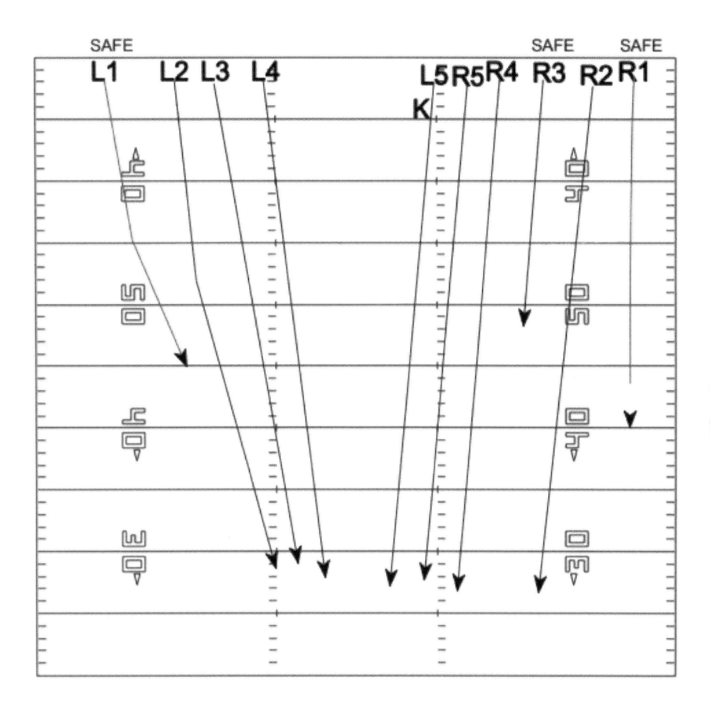

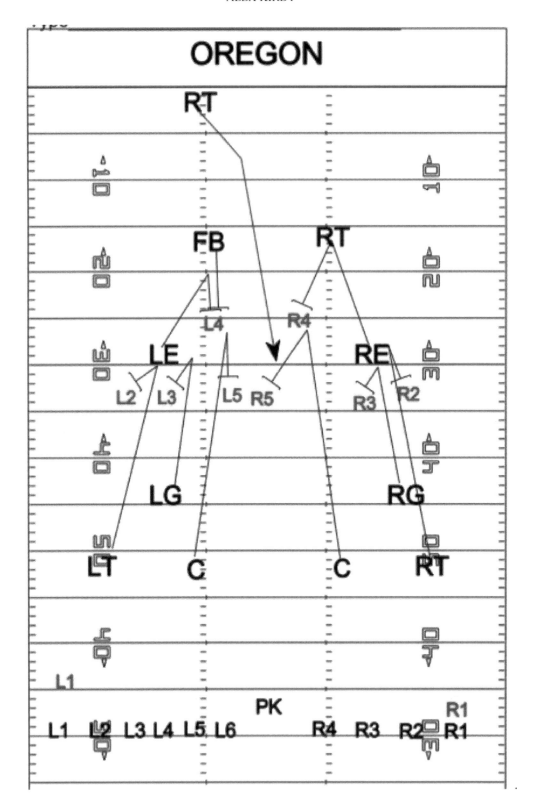

Oregon Drive 1 / Play 1 / 1ˢᵗ & 10 / -25 Yard Line / Left Hash / 15:00 1Q
Oregon 0 – OSU – 0
Summary
Mariota completes the pass to Byron Marshall for 8 yards to the left.

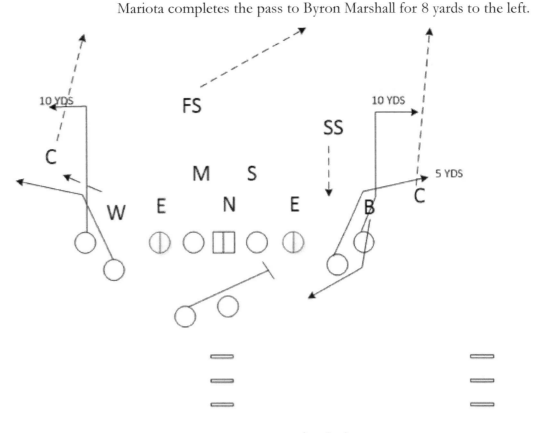

Analysis

On the first play, you see Oregon line up in a tight 2×2 set, with the receivers squeezed in together, and it's all about the leverage to the outside. Mariota is looking first to the flat route.

Ohio State lines up in an odd front with the defensive end standing up over the #2 receiver and playing the flat to that side. The alignment of the stand-up defensive end inside of the stacked receivers makes it pretty easy to get the flat route open. The defense is showing the threat of the edge pressure coming from the short side of the field. This gets the offense to slide the offensive line to the boundary side because of the threat.

Since the corner starts to sink to the deep third in cover 3, Mariota knows that the outside linebacker to that side is responsible for the flat to the boundary. The outside linebacker in question is walled-off (or picked, depending on your perspective) by the outside receiver going vertical, so the slot receiver will trail him and go underneath to the flat, wide open as you can see on the first play.

The play fake and the threat of the run, even before the ball is snapped, forces the defense to play its LBs so tight, that they cannot afford to cheat and provide extra leverage to the outside of the formation.

When the ball is snapped, Oregon gets an easy completion, and the offensive staff gets a good idea of how the Buckeyes will play this formation later on in the game.

<u>Oregon Drive 1/ Play 2 / 2nd & 2 / -33 Yard Line / Left Hash / 14:55 1Q</u>
Oregon 0 – OSU – 0

<u>Summary</u>
Pass complete to Byron Marshall for a gain of 8 yards and a first down.

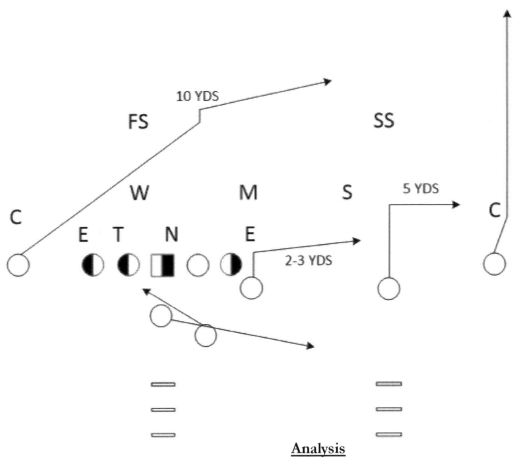

<u>Analysis</u>

The Ducks quickly line back up, this time in a 3×1 set with the strength to the field. The boot fake holds the defense long enough for Mariota to find a receiver out in the flat.

This is the "speed dial" approach to offense, which Oregon loves to do after picking up a first down.

This play stretches the underneath coverage, and the progression is outside-in, while keeping an eye on the corner to the wide side of the field, so against a hard corner in the flat, the Z receiver should look for the ball in the space between the corner and the safety at 12-15 yards.

It also helps to set up the run scheme that is designed to cut back to the tight end side. The thought is that the threat of the pass will keep the defenders to the trips side a little wider and create more space.

Oregon Drive 1 / Play 3 / 1ˢᵗ & 10 / -41 Yard Line / Left Hash / 14:46 1Q
Oregon 0 – OSU 0
Summary
Gain of 4 yards on the run up the middle.

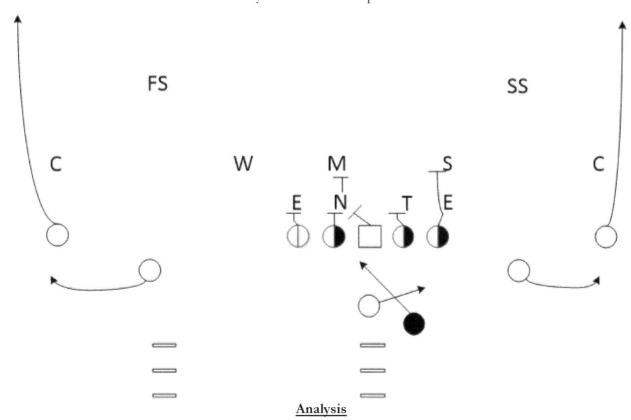

Analysis
Next up, Oregon lines up in a regular 2×2 set with the tight end flexed out, and a 5 on 5 look in the box. If the outside linebackers played a bit tighter, there's a good chance Mariota throws one of the bubble routes. As it stands, Scott Frost has found a way to get a numbers advantage inside, at least for the first four yards. This is a really good look for Oregon, since the defense is out of position against this set.

The back reads the guard in front of him working against the three technique defensive tackle, and the lack of a running lane to the front side forces the back to cut back to the field.

The key to the left side is the is the head up defensive end who forces the play outside to an unblocked outside linebacker. The right tackle gives the defensive end some token resistance before moving to the 2nd level and blocking out on the outside linebacker.

Oregon Drive 1 / Play 4 / 2nd & 6 / -45 Yard Line / Right Middle Hash / 14:31 1Q
Oregon 0 – OSU 0

Summary
Gain of 12 yards on the run. Ball carrier fumbles but recovers the ball on a fortunate bounce.

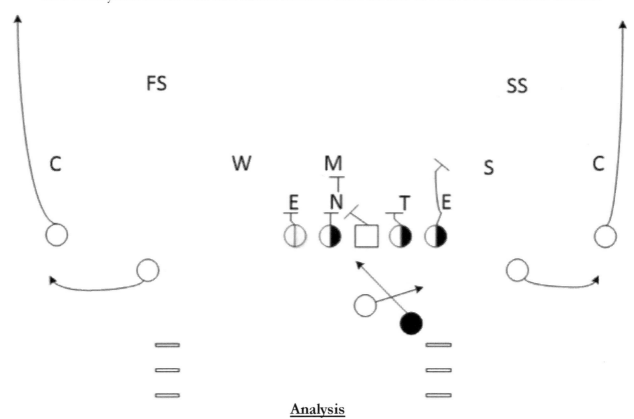

Analysis

Nothing new here, the Ducks will line up and run the exact same play over again, because they've got the numbers advantage inside that they want. One of the easiest ways to "hack" your way to a no-huddle offense is simply having a way to repeat the play call.

Scott Frost saw a potential running lane develop kind of late on the last play since the three technique fought his way across the face of the right guard and the Mike linebacker aggressively flowed to the offensive left side which opened up a huge running lane to the offensive right side.

The exact same thing happens this time, and on this play the back stays more patient and waits for a huge running lane to develop in the B gap. Every interior defender is sealed off and it's an even better result this time, as the back picks up twelve yards, and a first down.

Oregon Drive 1 / Play 5 / 1st & 10 / +43 Yard Line / Right Hash / 14:18 1Q
Oregon 0 – OSU 0
Summary
Gain of six yards up the middle.

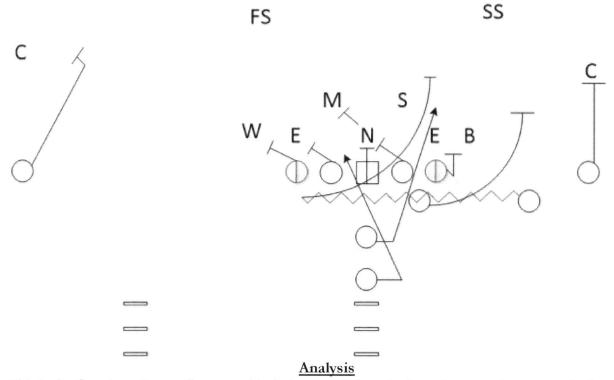

Analysis

This is the first time Oregon lines up with their strength into the boundary in order to get a look at how Ohio State will line up against the formation into the short side of the field. The offense motions back to a full-house formation and the coaching staff analyzes the reaction from the defensive front.

At the same time, they put the man in motion to watch the reaction from the defense to see if that provides them any advantage.

This is a second-level read with a "follow" blocker coming through the hole should Mariota choose to keep it. The back lines up in a tight pistol alignment behind the QB, and at the snap opens up like he's headed to the boundary, then reverses course and gets to the mesh point with Mariota. Reading the linebacker means that the offense has an extra man coming through the hole that the defense can't account for.

Oregon Drive 1 / Play 6 / 2nd & 4 / +37 Yard Line / Right Middle Hash / 13:57 1Q
Oregon 0 – OSU 0

Summary
Gain of 6 yards on the run for a first down.

Analysis

Not much new here except for the stacked alignments of the receivers to the outside. Scott Frost wants to press every advantage, and forcing the Buckeyes to declare with their alignment what they want to defend ends up putting only five Ohio State defenders in the box once again.

The defense doesn't align much differently than the four receiver look that the offense came out with earlier in the drive.

Oregon Drive 1 / Play 7 / 1st & 10 / +31 Yard Line / Left Middle / 13:41 1Q
Oregon 0 – OSU 0

Summary
Gain of 7 yards on the run up the middle by Mariota

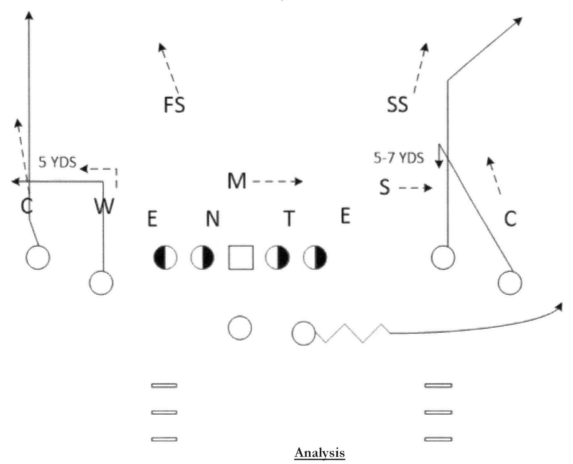

Analysis

On this play, Oregon decides to motion to an empty set for the first time, and essentially turns the right side of the formation into a bunch set. The motion takes the middle linebacker out of the middle of the field, so now the Oregon staff knows they can come back to this set later on in the game if they want to run a QB draw or some kind of pass that attacks the middle of the field.

Ohio State also leaves the corner route in single coverage with only the safety covering the deep outside leverage on the corner route. Oregon undoubtedly takes note of how Ohio State covers the bunch concept, and makes a note for later on in the game.

The Mike linebacker conspicuously chases the motion man, which allows Mariota to look to the left side of the field. There's nothing open to the left side of the field so he decides to take off, and nearly fumbles as he's tackled.

Oregon Drive 1 / Play 8 / 2nd & 3 / +24 Yard Line / Left Hash / 13:16 1Q
Oregon 0 – OSU 0
Summary
Pass complete for a gain of 7 yards and a first down.

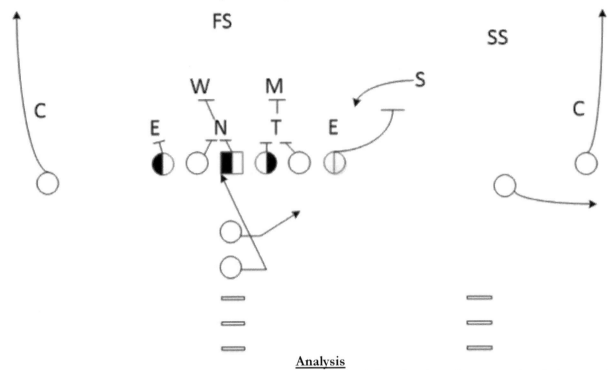

Analysis

On this play, Oregon lines up with an "attached" tight end for the first time, meaning he's not off the line of scrimmage or flexed out. This changes how the defense will align, if only slightly. It also forces the Sam LB to take seriously the perimeter run threat to that side, and puts him in conflict.

The Sam linebacker comes off the edge and comes inside of the tight end's block, which forces Mariota to get rid of the ball before he intended.

This is where the bubble route packaged with the zone read comes in handy where it essentially turns into a triple option.

Mariota manages to get the ball away, and Oregon has another first down.

The defense is in a Cover 6 look with a pressed corner to the boundary

Oregon Drive 1 / Play 9 / 1st & 10 / +18 Yard Line / Right Hash / 13:08 1Q
Oregon 0 – OSU 0
Summary
Gain of 2 yards on the run

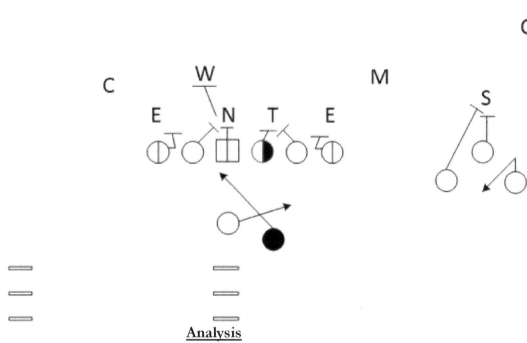

Analysis

On this play, Oregon lines up with an unbalanced set to the boundary, handing it off on the inside zone. The defensive line forces the running back to cut back, where the Mike linebacker is waiting for him.

What's important here is that not only did Oregon manage to make two yards out of essentially nothing, but also that they now have some idea of how Ohio State will line up to an unbalanced formation.

Oregon Drive 1 / Play 10 / 2nd & 8 / +15 Yard Line / Right Hash / 12:52 1Q

Oregon 0 – OSU 0

Summary

Gain of 8 yards on the run to the right by Mariota and a first down.

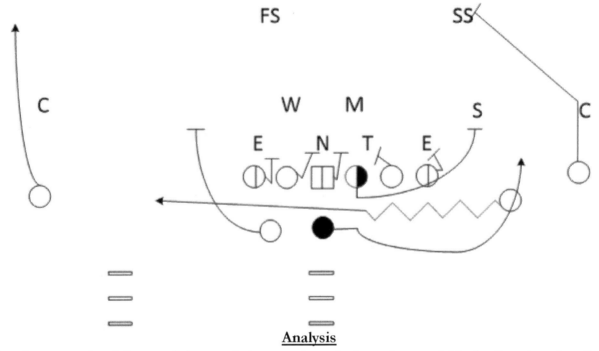

Analysis

Another example of Oregon lining up their strength to the boundary, and it's the first time that Oregon has used jet motion to hold defenders in place to run toward the opposite edge. This means that the motion keeps the defense from playing aggressively downhill into the gap.

In this case, they're going to fake the jet sweep to the field, with Mariota keeping the ball and following the guards around the edge to pick up a first down.

The defense is expecting something back to the field in this case (like the jet sweep) because offenses will play games with formations, trying to force the defense to commit extra men to the boundary, so that they can get the ball to the wide side of the field with fewer defenders to worry about.

Oregon Drive 1 / Play 11 / 1st & Goal / +7 Yard Line / Right Hash / 12:31 1Q
Oregon 0 – OSU 0
Summary

TOUCHDOWN! Pass complete from Mariota to the back left of the end zone for a gain of seven yards and a score.

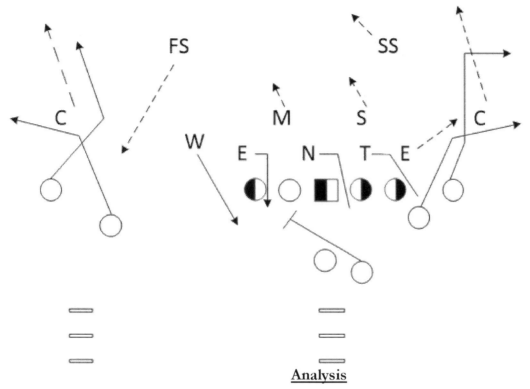

Analysis

The final play of the drive- the scoring play- comes about for a couple of reasons.

Oregon uses Ohio State's defensive game plan against them. The #2 receiver runs to the flat, which widens the corner, since he's in a Cover 3 scheme and has to play high and outside while the free safety heads to play the flat.

Secondly, Mariota's mobility inside the pocket buys time, and actually opens up throwing lanes down the field. As you can see, the free safety actually starts to come up when Mariota is scrambling around and avoiding the rush, as do the linebackers. As a result, the corner to the field side ends up defending two receivers, and the inside receiver is wide open in the middle of the field for the score.

Mariota does a fantastic job in this game of keeping his eyes down the field while scrambling around, and they score a touchdown because of it.

He originally intends to throw the flat route to the boundary side, but the dropping DE cuts off the throwing lane.

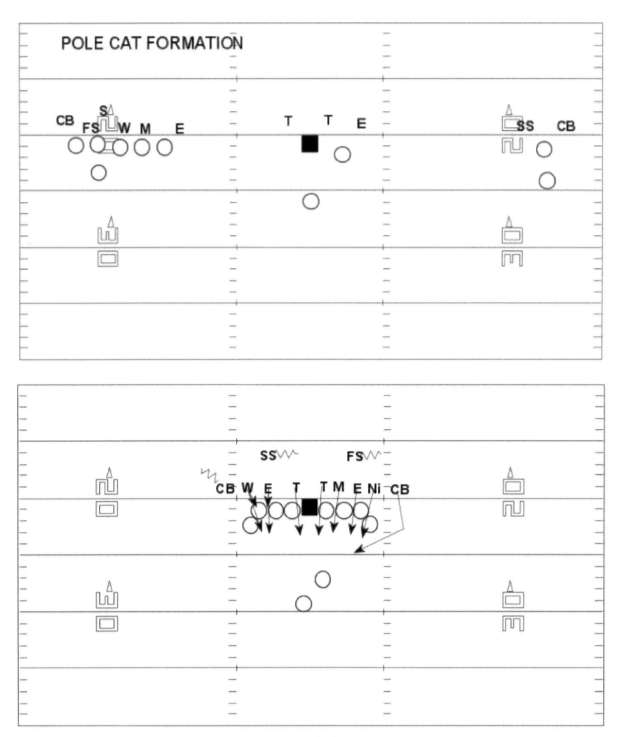

Analysis

Oregon lines up in the same polecat formation that they scored a two-point conversion on during the Rose Bowl, but Ohio State defends it correctly and the Ducks revert back to their more conventional PAT formation.

Instead of requiring the holder making the decision on whether to run a fake to count each member of the defense, he is just assigned to watch a certain defender, in this case, he's watching #97 from Ohio State. If goes wide to cover his man, that's an indicator that the defense is lined up correctly and the fake probably won't work. If he stays inside, you know that the defense is outnumbered and it's a good idea to go for two.

Oregon Drive #1 Review

Oregon

- Oregon plays with the alignments of the outside linebackers with 2x2 formations.
- They used motion to attack the middle of the field and create bunch concepts.
- Attacked the middle of the formation by spreading the defense.
- Mild success in the run game, and aside from one big play Ohio State has done a pretty good job of keeping the ground attack contained.

Ohio State

- Ohio State kept it pretty simple on this drive by playing with a base 4-3 look and two-deep much of the drive, and an odd front edge pressure as well.
- Against 2x2 formations the Buckeyes are playing their outside linebackers in a halfway position to split the difference between the offensive tackle and the slot receiver in order to play the bubble routes and the run game.
- So far, they're putting a 3 and a 5 technique to the side of the back in one-back formations, and a head-up defensive end over the offensive tackle to the opposite side.

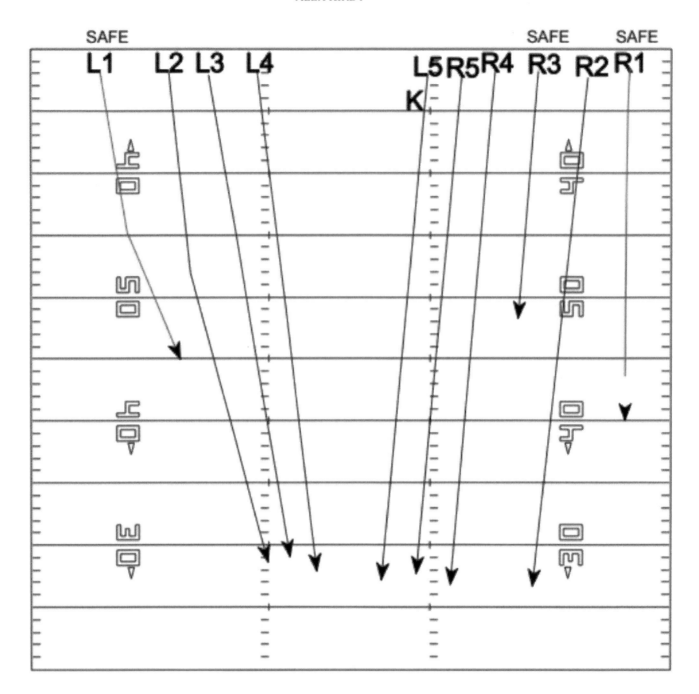

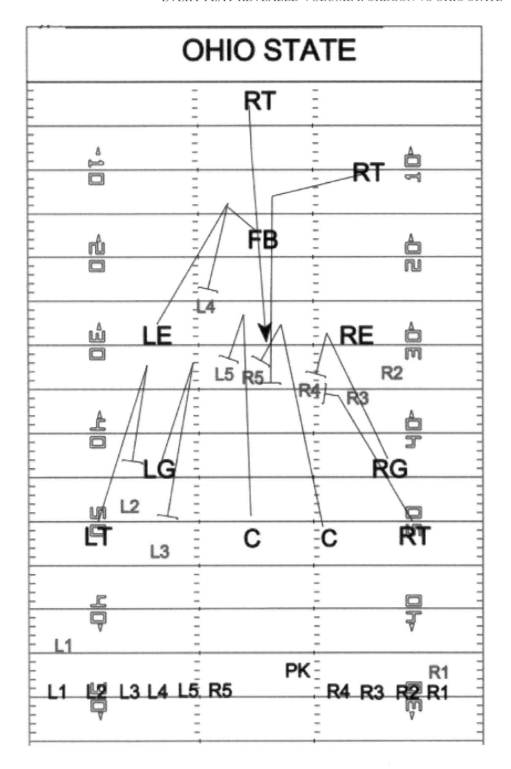

<u>Ohio State Drive 1 / Play 1 / 1st & 10 / -25 Yard Line / Right Hash / 12:21 1Q</u>

Oregon 7 – OSU 0

<u>Summary</u>

Gain of 2 yards on the run up the middle.

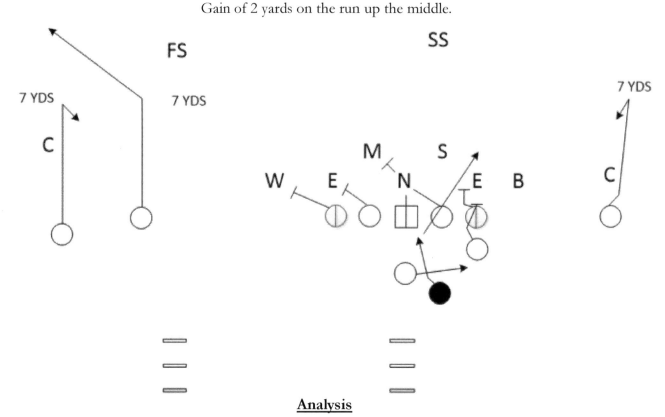

<u>Analysis</u>

Ohio State gets the defense to flinch on the first play of the game by forcing them to show their intentions early, as the safety to the short side of the field is lined up at linebacker depth, and who quickly retreats back to his normal depth once Ohio State changes the play at the line of scrimmage. It's likely that Ohio State is expecting some kind of pressure from the short side of the field.

Cardale changes up the formation, puts the tight end behind the right tackle and the back set to the same side. Almost like a split zone because the offensive line moved away from the tight end to the field, and looked like the tight end was folding under the right tackle to get to the backside inside linebacker.

Ohio State Drive 1 / Play 2 / 2nd & 8 / -27 Yard Line / Right Hash / 12:09 1Q

Oregon 7 – OSU 0

Summary

Gain of 4 yards on the run by Cardale Jones.

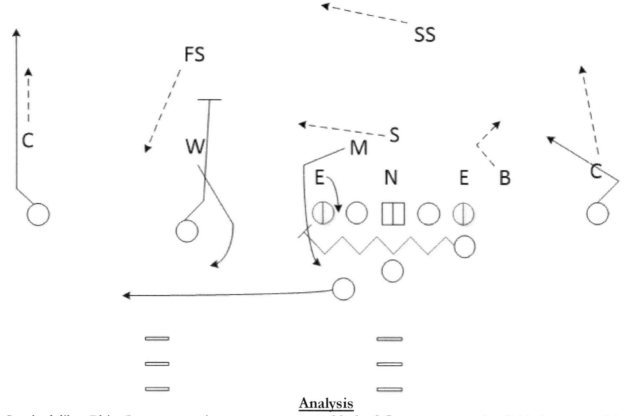

Analysis

Looked like Ohio State was trying to set up some kind of flare screen to the field there, possibly in response to a field blitz that they already knew was coming before Oregon did it.

The X receiver on the right side doesn't do a great job of giving Cardale a second option when the flare route is pretty well covered by the defense, so he's forced to take off around the corner to the boundary side for four yards.

This kind of play is one of the easiest ways to get the ball out in space to one of their best athletes, but Oregon reacts pretty well.

Ohio State Drive 1 / Play 3 / 3rd & 4 / -31 Yard Line / Right Hash / 11:47 1Q
Oregon 7 – OSU – 0
Summary
Cardale Jones runs for 6 yards and a first down.

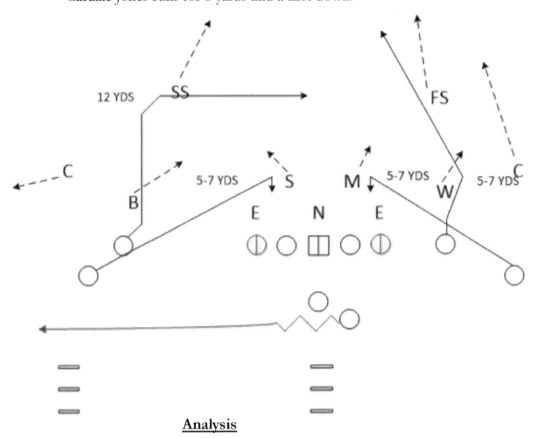

Analysis

Ohio State lines up in a 2x2 set with the back motioning out to the field to form a bunch look at the snap.

Oregon drops eight into coverage, but Cardale picks up the first down with his legs. The strong outside linebacker (B) funnels the two receivers stacked to that side of the field, leaving only the corner available to take the flare in the flat. Offense runs two drag-hook routes into the middle as well as a post/dig concept to challenge a single safety but there are four underneath defenders muddying up the short middle, meaning that the safeties can easily handle the deep route to their side.

The flare route is actually wide open, but Cardale can't see him and had to take off as the pass rush got close.

<u>Ohio State Drive 1 / Play 4 / 1st & 10 / -37 Yard Line / Middle / 11:23 1Q</u>

Oregon 0 – OSU 7

Summary

Elliott runs for 3 yards

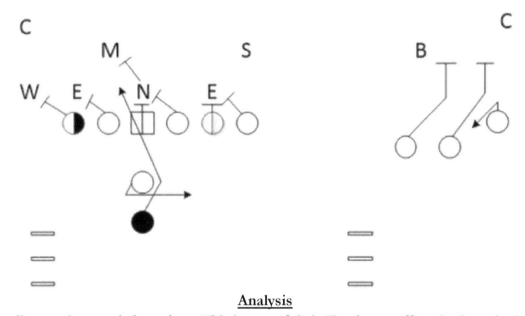

<u>Analysis</u>

Ohio State lines up in an unbalanced set. This is part of their "Lookover offense" where they run inside zone to the weak side because they are equal blockers vs defenders (not counting the corner). The backside inside linebacker is stacked wider and in a position to scrape on the quarterback in case of a keeper.

An attached tight end in the formation is a very reliable indicator that a run is coming, especially out of an unbalanced set like this one.

Ohio State Drive 1 / Play 5 / 2ⁿᵈ & 7 / -40 Yard Line / Middle / 10:49 1Q
Oregon 7 – OSU 0
Summary
Pass complete to the flare route for no gain.

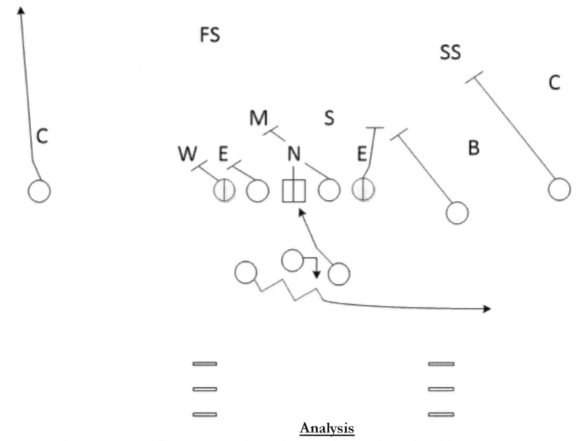

Analysis

Two-back gun twins with an opposite back flare motion to the twins side. This appears to be the classic inside zone with a flare screen coming off of it, however the one big adjustment to the scheme is that the right tackle comes off the line of scrimmage and releases down the field in an attempt to get a hand on the inside linebacker flying out to the flat to cover the flare motion.

In this case, the offense is mistakenly relying the back to make the unblocked outside linebacker miss, but the back is stopped after a minimal gain.

Ohio State Drive 1 / Play 6 / 3ʳᵈ & 7 / -40 Yard Line / Right Hash / 10:13 1Q
Oregon 7 – OSU 0
Summary
Gain of 2 yards on the scramble by Cardale Jones

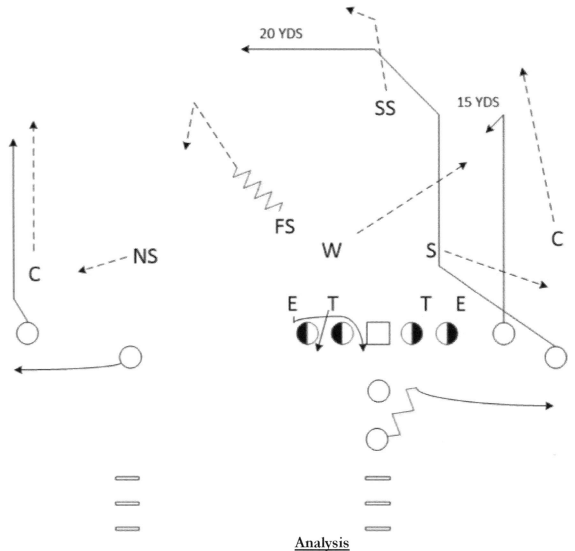

Analysis

Cardale is responsible for reading the defense's drop to the short side of the field, and whether or not they cover the curl and the dig route will determine whether or not he's able to find an open receiver or take off like he does in this example.

The defense is in a cover 6 look, with the quarters side to the field. This explains why the free safety is able to come downhill so quickly and put a stop to Cardale's scramble and stop him short of the first down.

SKY PUNT

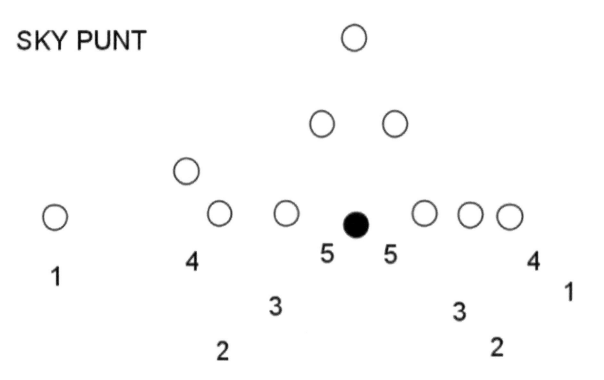

Analysis

Urban Meyer's first goal on any drive is to get to the 40 yard line, since he feels that at this point he should have the ability to flip the field on the opponent. This is a big reason why he feels he can be so aggressive in the open field area, since he already has the ability to pin them deep inside their territory, which is exactly what happens on this play.

OREGON PUNT RETURN FORMATIONS

8 HOLD

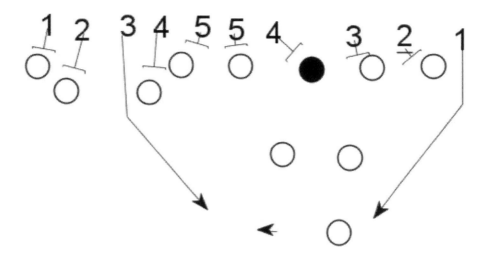

Analysis

Oregon's intention is to press the coverage players at the line of scrimmage and help set up a return coming back the other way.

Ohio State Drive #1 Review

<u>Ohio State</u>

This offense kept mixing up formations early and often in this drive, giving the defense unbalanced formations, two-back sets, moving the tight end around, and making an effort to get the football out wide to the back in the flat.

During the drive, the offense used zone schemes exclusively up front against this odd front from Oregon, never pulling any linemen.

<u>Oregon</u>

The Ducks stayed pretty basic on defense, only bringing any real pressure one time. For the most part they focused on staying gap sound and getting a feel for the kinds of things that Ohio State wanted to do.

Oregon Drive 2 / Play 1 / 1ˢᵗ & 10 / -11 Yard Line / Right Hash / 9:10 1Q
Oregon 7 – OSU 0

Summary
Pass complete for a gain of 28 yards and a first down to the shallow crossing route over the middle.

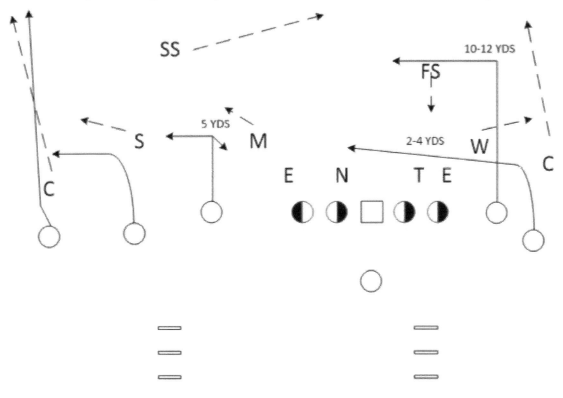

Analysis

Oregon lines up in an empty formation, looks like a stick concept to the 3 WR side, with a drive concept coming from the boundary. Will backer widens out to the boundary flat at the snap, is rubbed by the #2 receiver going vertical.

Note that the Mike linebacker isn't lined up too wide, but is outside of the defensive end to the field side, which is wide enough to cover the route by the #3 receiver and opens up the drive route coming in from the other side of the field.

Commonly referred to as "3 Buzz" coverage with the boundary safety coming to the middle of the field to replace the widening linebackers and stay gap sound against the run and anything the QB may try.

The free safety is in a decent position to make a tackle, but is picked by the umpire, resulting in the big gain. Defense lined up with 2 safeties trying to bait Mariota into throwing into the middle or running against a vacated middle of the field, then rotated to a single-high look.

Oregon Drive 2 / Play 2 / 1ˢᵗ & 10 / -38 Yard Line / Middle / 9:01 1Q
Oregon 7 – OSU 0
Summary

Gain of 4 yards on the run by Tyner.

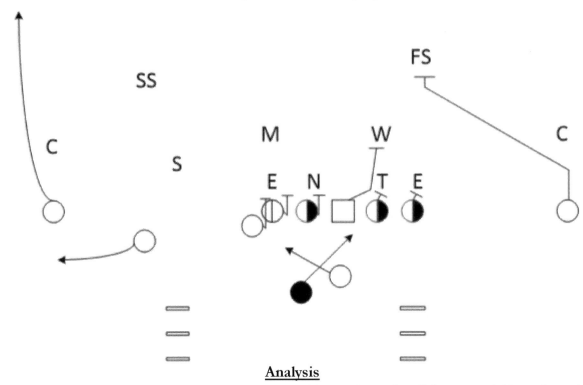

Analysis

Oregon lines up super-fast on this play in a trips Y-off look where they'll line up quickly and run inside zone to the weak side with the TE scooping and sealing off the potential QB player who was lined up wider to the side of the back.

The tailback tries extra hard to fit in the shallow space because he doesn't want to cut back to the unblocked outside linebacker.

Inside zone is a good play for them at this tempo because it allows the offensive line to move as one and limit the amount of open space in the middle of the offensive line, which can be particularly dangerous for an offense when a defense isn't lined up yet and the down linemen and linebackers aren't where they're supposed to be.

The backside tight end shuffles in step with the left tackle to eliminate any space and cut off the defensive end to that side.

Worth noting that the two inside defensive tackles flipped sides (not bumped, but flipped) before the play. One is the nose and one is the 3 tech.

Oregon Drive 2 / Play 3 / 2nd & 6 / -42 Yard Line / Middle / 8:47 1Q
Oregon 7 – OSU 0

Summary
Tyner gain of 3 yards on the run.

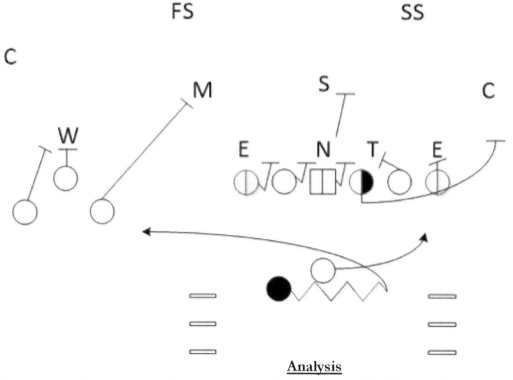

Analysis

Mariota is reading the defensive end over the left tackle, and in this situation the end hugs the hip of the offensive tackle, following the path of the offensive line. If the end had come straight up the field and cut off the path of the tailback, Mariota would've kept the ball and followed the guard around the edge.

Oregon lines up in a 3x1 bunch set and Ohio State is "clouding" (playing a hard corner) to the closed side of the formation. The outside linebacker to the 3 WR side is definitely the flat player, and the contain man, because he flew outside as soon as he read run from the blocking in front of him.

If the defense is clouding to the closed side, the corner doesn't do a good job of playing contain, since he doesn't seem to even try to get an angle on the puller moving to his side of the field.

<u>Oregon Drive 2 / Play 4 / 3rd & 3 / -45 Yard Line / Left Hash / 8:23 1Q</u>
Oregon 7 – OSU 0
<u>Summary</u>
Pass incomplete and Oregon has to punt.

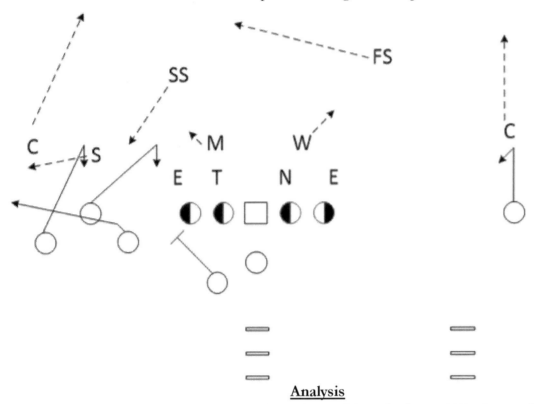

<u>Analysis</u>

Quick spacing concept to the boundary and it's dropped by a freshman WR. Oregon basically put four men into the boundary, though the back in the backfield just kicked out on the edge of quick protection.

The defense rolls to a cover 3 look again, this time to the boundary. This is a great adjustment against the bunch formation that's lined up into the boundary.

Backside receiver runs a simple hitch at five yards.

This is why Ohio State doesn't press the "point" of the bunch, so that they can give themselves a big enough cushion to lock in on the same guy and not have to switch coverage responsibilities because of being picked by receivers or other defenders. The Sam stays over #3 and plays man coverage to the flat.

OREGON PUNT FORMATIONS

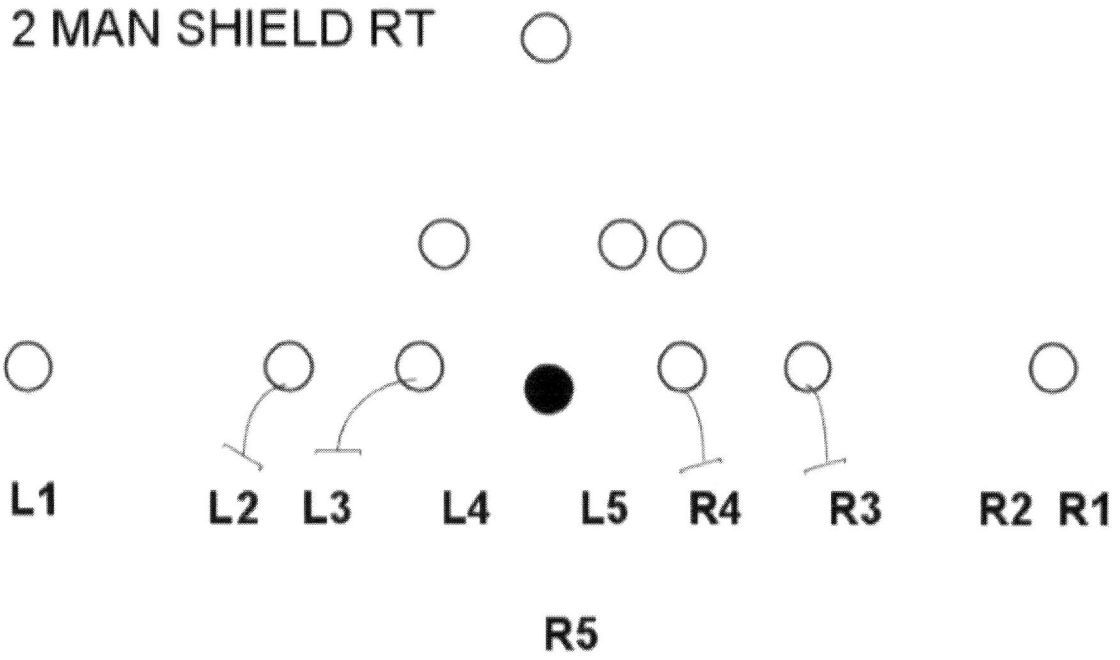

2 MAN SHIELD RT

L1   L2 L3   L4   L5   R4   R3   R2 R1

R5

SAFE RET

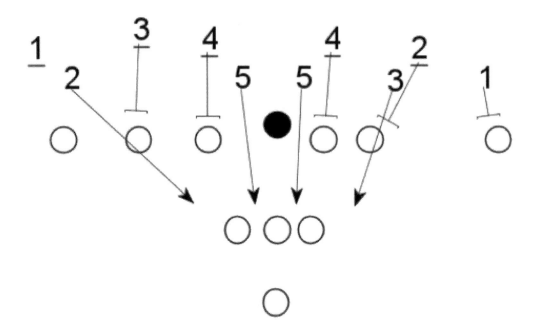

Oregon Drive #2

Oregon

A drive stopped short by an easily-avoidable mistake when a receiver drops a pass. Oregon uses four different formations, attacking different areas of the field with perimeter runs. Still, they manage to get the past the 40 yard line to put the punt team in a good position to flip the field.

Ohio State

The defense has been let off the hook on this drive, but they've got some issues in pass coverage, particularly when it comes to defending underneath passes that come open because of the offense creating rubs on defenders.

Ohio State Drive 2 / Play 1 / 1ˢᵗ & 10 / -3 Yard Line / Right Hash / 7:52 1Q
Oregon 7 – OSU 0
Summary
Gain of 2 yards by Cardale Jones

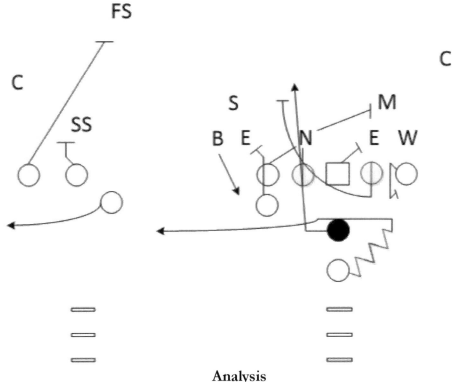

Analysis

Ohio State comes out in an unbalanced receiver set that Oregon came out with the week before.

The weak side outside linebacker tightens down over the backside tackle to a head up four technique. OSU runs a QB power with a Jet fake. I think Oregon may have been trying to bring field pressure here, or at least the strong outside linebacker, and the safeties lined up pretty similarly to how FSU defended the formation the week before in the Rose Bowl.

The defensive end to the playside is so quick that he runs all the way around the kickout block of the H-back and manages to get a hand on the QB, and the defensive end to the opposite side comes over the top of the combo block and also helps on the tackle.

The free safety is completely removed from the run strength of the formation by the alignment of the "bunch" of unbalanced receivers.

Ohio State Drive 2 / Play 2 / 2nd & 8 / -5 Yard Line / Right Middle / 7:40 1Q
Oregon 7 – OSU 0
Summary
Incomplete pass as Cardale Jones throws the ball away.

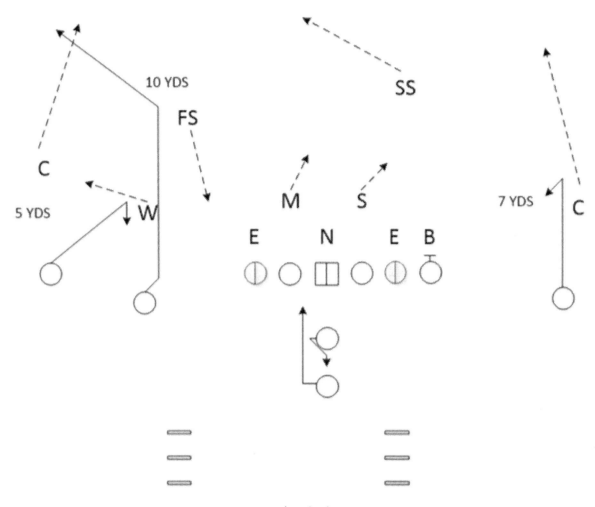

Analysis

Cardale gets flushed out of the pocket by Arik Armstead at the defensive end position, and ends up throwing the ball away.

This is a classic smash concept to the two receiver side, with a lone hitch route from the Z receiver to the opposite side of the formation that should be hot against a blitz.

This is an interesting adjustment by the secondary for Oregon. It's a common adjustment against teams who run a lot of the smash concept, where the overhang defender will play the underneath route man-to-man, and the corner will try to take away the corner route with outside leverage.

Cardale is coached up to read the corner, and when the corner drops to the deep third, the outside linebacker plays man-to-man on the X receiver, playing with inside leverage on the route in order to cut off the throw, since the defense is trying to trick the quarterback into throwing the hitch route. At the same time, the corner will drop to the deep third and open up to play outside leverage on any outside-breaking routes.

Ohio State Drive 2 / Play 3 / 3rd & 8 / -5 Yard Line / Right Middle / 7:11 1Q
Oregon 7 – OSU 0
Summary
Pass complete for 26 yards and a first down.

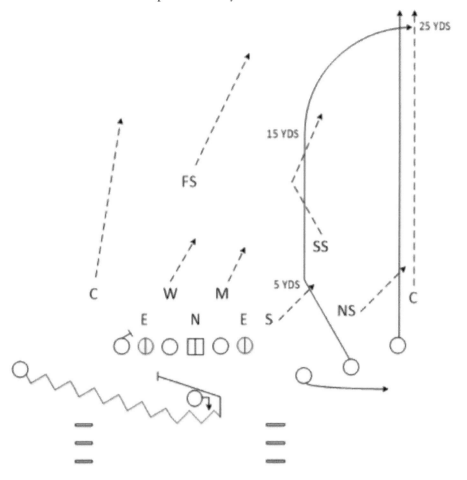

Analysis

This is a perfect play for third and long against a defense that doesn't like to bring a lot of pressure. The offense lines up in an empty set with the tailback split out wide, then brings him into the backfield so that the offense is lined up in a 3x1 formation with a closed side aligned to the field. The Oregon defense lines up with nickel personnel, which should, in theory at least, make it tougher on Ohio State to pass the ball.

The outside receiver runs vertical, and the #3 receiver runs a bubble route which occupies the flat defender. The Free Safety stays deep and doubles the vertical route by #1, and the only time anyone in the secondary even gets a hand on the #2 receiver who ends up making the catch is when the strong safety manages to grab him as he's making his outside break to the sideline.

The offense is attacking the deep right side, and even in a long-yardage situation, this is an incredibly deep route by the #2 receiver, and his job is to replace the space vacated by the corner. With no pressure whatsoever, Cardale has lots of time to wait for the deep out route to come open and he puts the ball right on the money.

<u>Ohio State Drive 2 / Play 4 / 1st & 10 / -31 Yard Line / Right Hash / 7:03 1Q</u>
Oregon 7 – OSU 0
<u>Summary</u>
Pass complete to Marshall for 26 yards and a first down.

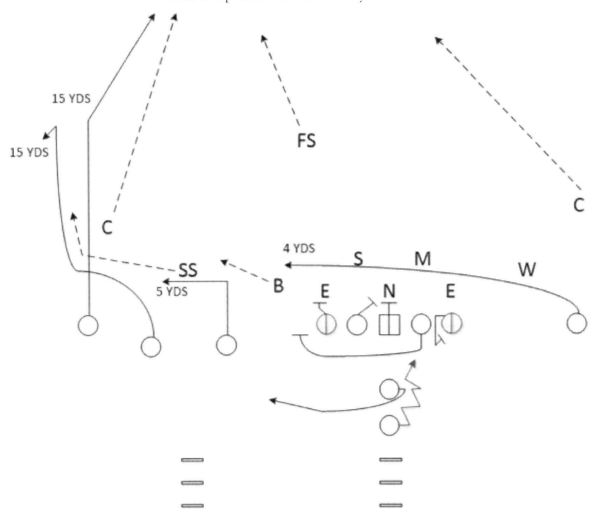

<u>Analysis</u>

This concept attacks the wide side of the field at three different levels, with the outside receiver running the deep post, breaking in at 15-17 yards, the wheel route, which breaks up the field at the top of the numbers at a five yard depth, and the out route at five yards.

Once the corner sees #1 go outside to the flat he turns his shoulder and it turns into man coverage with the corner's back to the QB. By trailing the post route, he opens up some space at the sideline, which consequently opens up space in the flat for the #3 receiver.

Cardale puts the ball on the inside shoulder of the receiver, but the receiver does a great job of adjusting to the pass and making a great catch on the sideline.

Ohio State Drive 2 / Play 5 / 1ˢᵗ & 10 / +43 Yard Line / Left Hash / 6:40 1Q
Oregon 7 – OSU 0
Summary
Ezekiel Elliott runs for a gain of 1 yard.

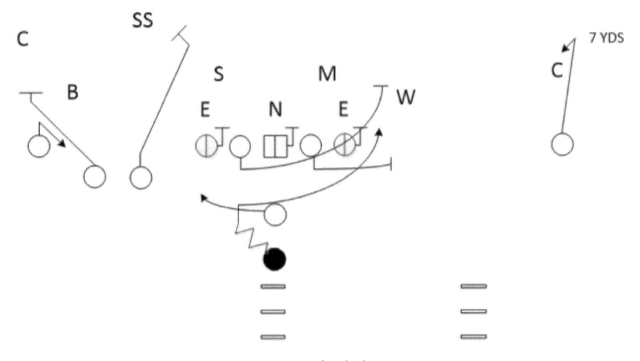

Analysis

The front side guard doesn't have great balance on the edge, which makes it easier for the Will backer to shed the block and force the cutback on the play. The failed block on the front side of the play screws up the path of the backside guard, meaning that the two pullers lose all momentum and space to the front side, and forcing the back to cut back into the Sam linebacker who is waiting there.

The play is packaged with a hitch screen from the three receiver side into the boundary, and a single hitch route that's hot against any kind of field pressure on the opposite side of the field.

Even if they never run this play again, Ohio State has forced Oregon to account for the pin and pull scheme to the open side of the formation.

Ohio State Drive 2 / Play 6 / 2nd & 11 / +42 Yard Line / Left Middle / 6:16 1Q
Oregon 7 – OSU 0
Summary
Incomplete pass

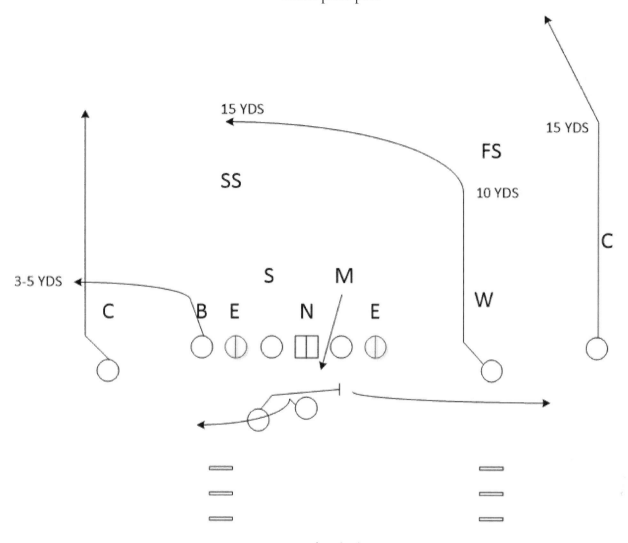

Analysis

The key to this play is that the crossing route by the slot receiver is not disrupted by the outside linebacker to his side, however since the receiver doesn't make his break to the middle until he gets to about 10 yards depth, Cardale can't get him the ball, no matter how wide open he may be. He also can't wait for the crossing route to come open, and shrugs off the linebacker blitzing through the B gap. Once he clears the pressure, the only route left open is the flare to the wide side of the field.

The nose tackle does a good job of occupying both the center and the right guard to clear up open space in the interior for the blitzing linebacker.

Ohio State Drive 2 / Play 7 / 3rd & 9 / +42 Yard Line / Left Hash / 5:47 1Q
Oregon 7 – OSU 0

Summary
Cardale Jones runs for 7 yards.

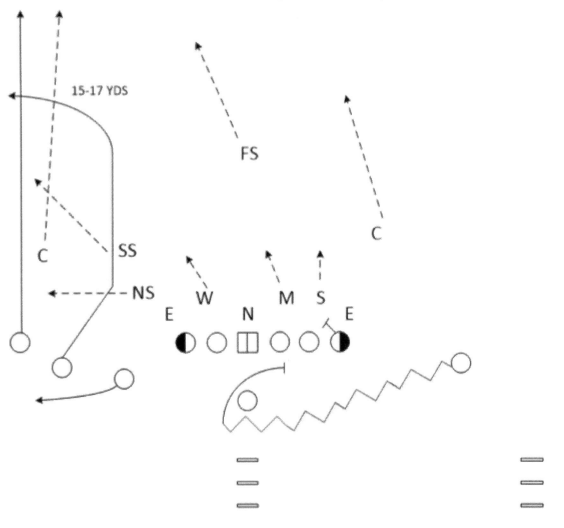

Analysis

This is basically the same 3rd and long play that Ohio State used earlier on the drive, with the sail route just being run about ten yards shallower. Oregon's defense appears to have made an adjustment to this formation, setting their strength to the passing strength into the boundary, and putting the extra defensive back in a position to defend against out-breaking routes to the sideline.

With his primary and secondary receivers covered, Cardale sees an open lane and nearly picks up the first down with his feet.

Ohio State Drive 2 / Play 8 / 4th & 2 / +35 Yard Line / Left Hash / 5:32 1Q

Oregon 7 – OSU 0

Summary

Jet sweep to Marshall picks up 2 yards for the first down.

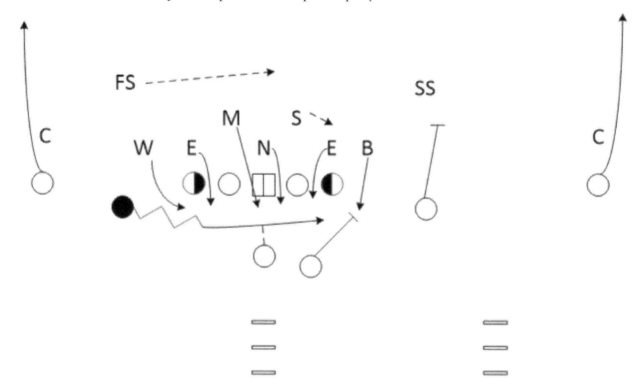

Analysis

Oregon actually does a decent job of defending this play by forcing the ball carrier back inside and bringing edge pressure from both sides. The design of the play allows the Sam linebacker to roam free without worrying about being blocked, since all gaps are filled by defenders.

The defense is in a cover 0 scheme, meaning that the safeties are manned-up on the slot receivers, which is why the free safety runs with the slot receiver in motion. The Mike linebacker shoots through the open A gap away from the play, and chases down the receiver on the jet sweep from behind when he has no more room to run to the front side.

He manages to put his head down and barely pick up the first down.

<u>Ohio State Drive 2 / Play 9 / 1st & 10 / +33 Yard Line / Right Hash / 5:02 1Q</u>
Oregon 7 – OSU 0
<u>Summary</u>
Incomplete pass.

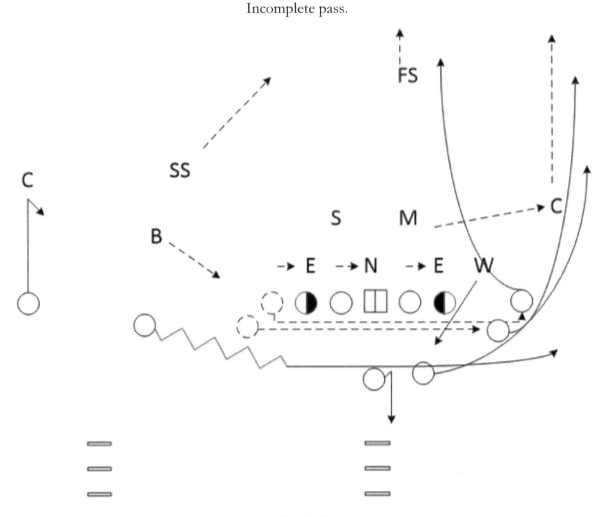

<u>Analysis</u>

Ohio State lines up in an unbalanced formation lined up to the field, then shifts their tight end and H-back to the boundary. The entire defensive front for Oregon shift along with them to the shades that are drawn up in the diagram above.

The idea behind this play, like several of the pass plays before, is to flood the short side of the field with receivers and find the open man. The first two receivers going vertical are both carried by the two defensive backs to that side of the field, but the Mike linebacker widening keeps his eyes in the backfield on the flare route, opening up a hole in the coverage for the wheel route from the backfield. The pass is just off the mark falling incomplete out of bounds.

Ohio State Drive 2 / Play 10 / 2nd & 10 / +33 Yard Line / Right Hash / 4:44 1Q

Oregon 7 – OSU 0

Summary

Touchdown! Ezekiel Elliot 33 yard run for a score.

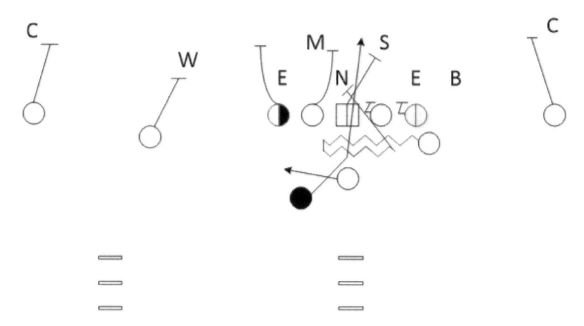

Analysis

This play is not necessarily designed to attack the nose tackle specifically, but the offensive line is instructed to trap the first down lineman on the play side past the center. With a very late stem by the nose to the left shoulder of the center, he now becomes the first down defender past the center. This means that the defensive end to the play side is unblocked, and the offensive line can block both inside linebackers, which is what springs this play for a big touchdown.

Since the defensive front is designed to force everything inside to these two inside backers, by sealing them off from the play the only men left to make a play on the runner are the safeties, who are out of position. The Mike linebacker is effectively doubled by both the left guard and the left tackle giving him nowhere to go.

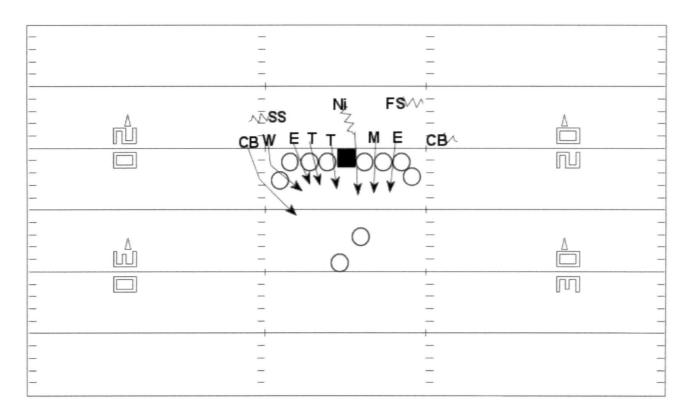

Analysis

When designing a protection and a PAT/FG block it's all about personnel and finding the individual matchups, especially on the edge against the wing on either side.

Ohio State Drive #2 Review

<u>Ohio State</u>

Unlike the previous drive, Ohio State uses a whole lot of gap schemes with pulling guards and continues to mix up formations.

The shift to the boundary tested Oregon's defense with regards to coverage and alignment.

The 98 yard drive takes a lot of air out of Oregon's defense, and helps set the tone for later on.

<u>Oregon</u>

Pass coverage was a big liability on this drive, and they still didn't bring much pressure.

They need to come up with answers for the offensive package featuring a tight end off the ball, as well as a way to free up their backside inside linebacker against gap schemes.

They also need answers for flood routes into the short side of the field, which is what killed them on 3rd and very long when Ohio State was backed up against their own end zone.

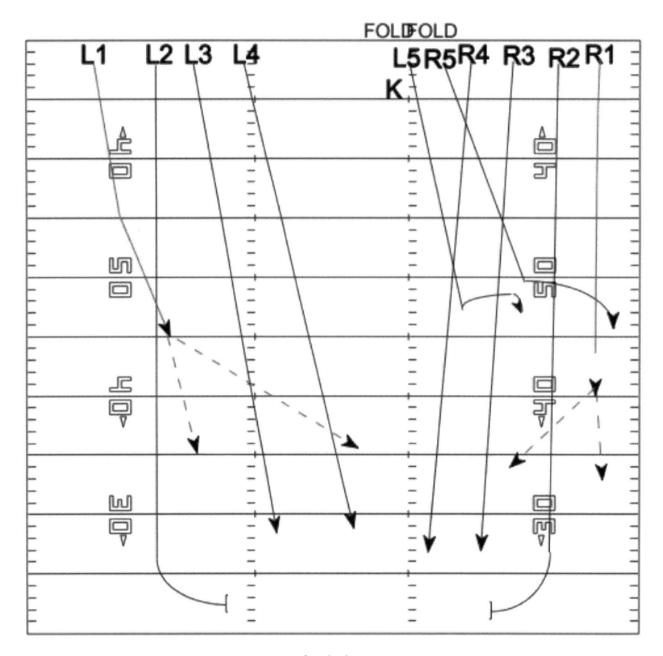

Analysis

This kickoff scheme is designed to get the ball to the inside of the offensive right hash.

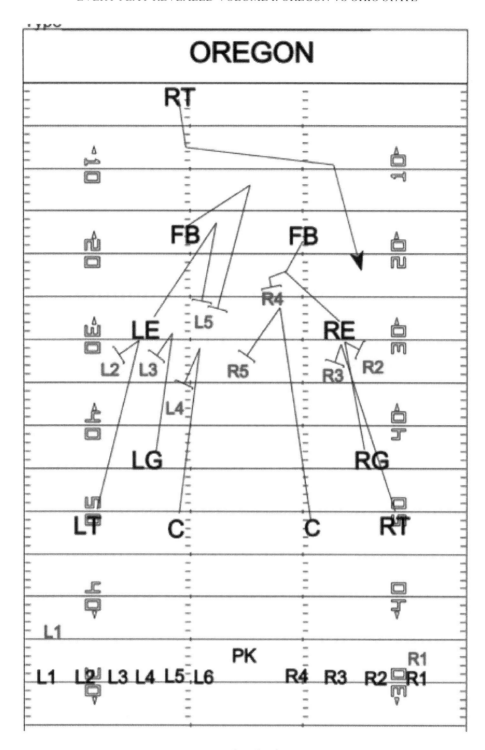

Analysis

The returner in this case is freelancing because there's more room outside. #35 for Oregon doesn't anticipate the return coming that way.

<u>Oregon Drive 3 / Play 1 / 1st & 10 / -17 Yard Line / Left Hash / 4:27 1Q</u>
Oregon 7 – OSU 7
Summary
Run for 8 yards.

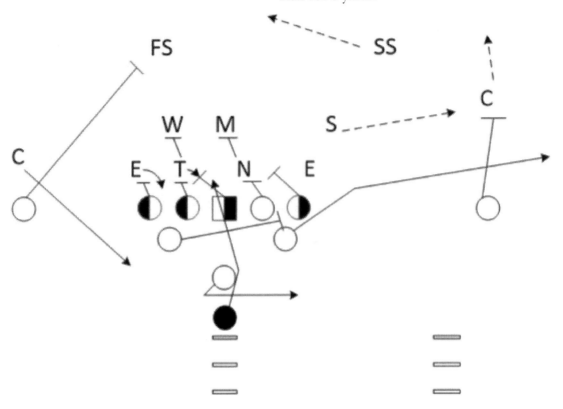

<u>Analysis</u>

The corner blitz is ill-timed and forces the cutback to the boundary, which is nothing but open grass because the corner comes so wide off the edge. It's a wham scheme where the front side back runs a flat route and brings the Sam backer with him to make the picture a little bit clearer to the right side. It's actually a pretty safe and gap sound way (most of the time) to be aggressive against the run game.

This is the first time Oregon has lined up in a formation with more than one back in the backfield. They've motioned to it before this drive, but lining up gives the defense more time to recognize the formation and make any appropriate checks.

Oregon wants to see if they can remove a guy from the box, or even find a way to get the ball on the edge.

Oregon Drive 3 / Play 2 / 2nd & 2 / -25 Yard Line / Left Hash / 4:17 1Q
Oregon 7 – OSU 7

Summary
Pass complete to Evan Baylis for a gain of 5 yards and a first down.

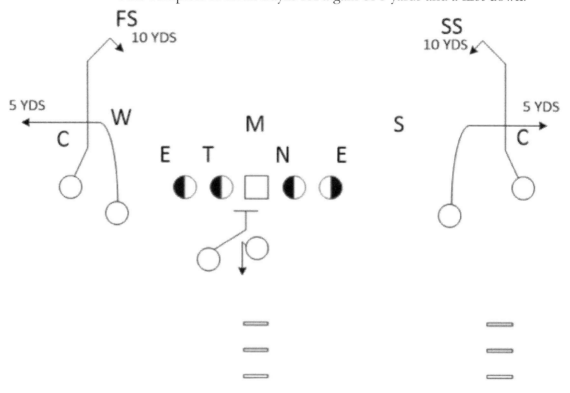

Analysis

This is the same principle as the play Oregon ran on the first play of the game. The corner is aggressively pressed on the outside receiver on both sides of the formation, and the X receiver's path on the left side walls off the outside linebacker from the flat route, making it an easy catch for the first down.

It's worth noting that right now Oregon, and even Ohio State is making a living throwing a short side of the field, especially on high-percentage plays like this one.

Oregon Drive 3 / Play 3 / 1ˢᵗ & 10 / -30 Yard Line / Left Hash / 4:02 1Q
Oregon 7 – OSU 7
Summary
Pass complete to Evan Baylis for a 1 yard gain.

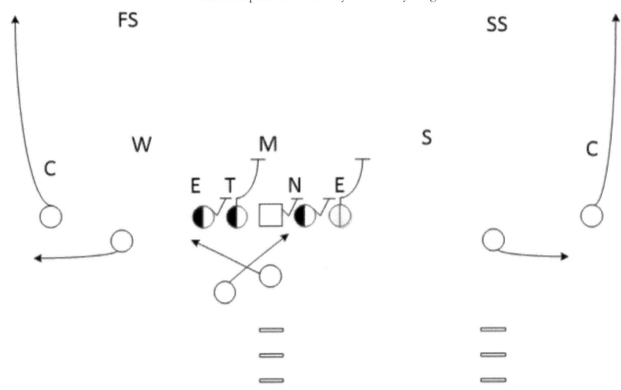

Analysis

Even though it's a 4-1 box, it's a pre-called zone read, so that the right tackle and right guard combo block out to the Sam in the alley. In this way the offense can put a body on the alley defender to that side in case the back is forced to bounce the play outside as has happened so many times before.

On this play, the bubble route to the boundary acts like a pitch man in the classic triple option. The free safety reads run right away and comes aggressively downhill.

The unblocked defensive end squeezes without committing himself to chasing the back, and forces Mariota to pull the football and the get it out to the slot receiver running the bubble route.

One unfortunate part of running this play is that it leaves the center one-on-one with the nose with no help.

Oregon Drive 3 / Play 4 / 2nd & 9 / -31 Yard Line / Left Hash / 3:46 1Q
Oregon 7 – OSU 7
Summary
Freeman run for a loss of 3 yards.

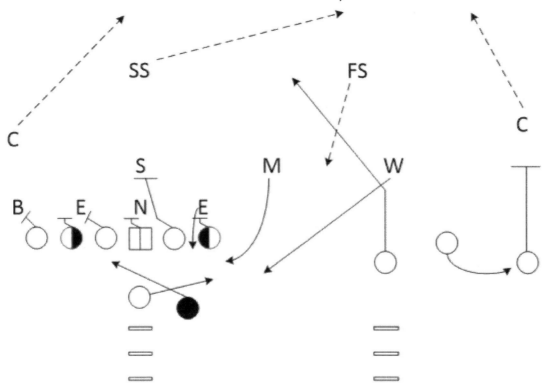

Analysis
The offense runs a stretch play to the boundary with the goal of cutting up inside of the tight end.

The defense brings two outside linebackers from the field, which allows the defensive line to slant across the face of the offensive linemen across from them and chase down the back, shutting down any hope of the stretch play working.

Even with the bubble and seam routes backside, it would be tough for Mariota to set up and throw it accurately to the wide side of the field with so much pressure in his face.

Oregon 3 / Play 5 / 3ʳᵈ & 13 / 27 Yard Line / Left Hash / 3:15 1Q
Oregon 7 – OSU 7
Summary
Pass incomplete.

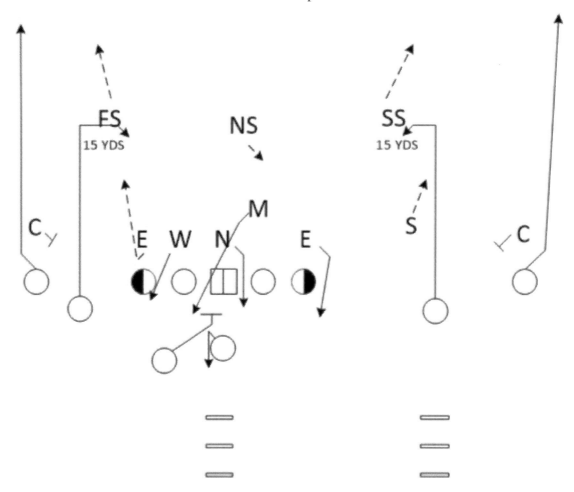

Analysis

The inside curl routes inside hold the safeties while the two outside receivers run vertical. The Z receiver gets wide open down the field because the safety to that side of the field is so occupied with the #2 receiver running an option route in his face, and getting in that open space behind the Sam linebacker dropping deep.

The secondary starts out in a 3-deep look as the nickel safety is standing in the middle of the field pre-snap, but the defense moves to a 2-deep look once the ball is snapped from center. The Z receiver is so incredibly wide open but he drops a sure pass and Oregon is forced to punt.

2 MAN SHIELD RT

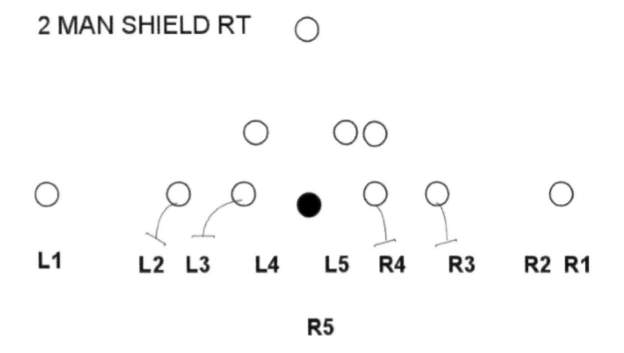

Analysis

The two gunners criss-cross coming down the field with the goal of seeking out the returner.

7 MAN BLOCK

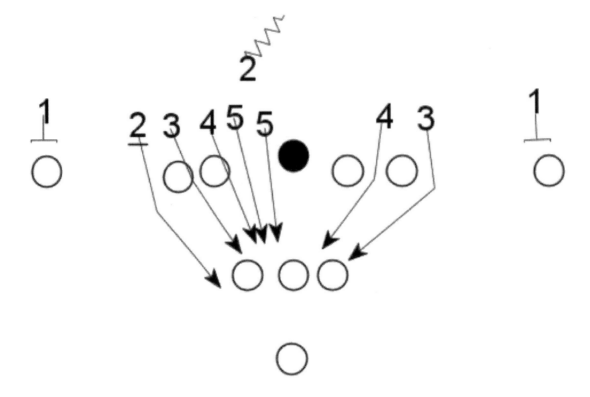

<u>Analysis</u>

The return scheme is designed to send a lot of pressure up the middle and hold up the punt coverage team.

Oregon Drive #3 Review

Oregon

It should be noted that the playaction fakes used on this drive were just as much about timing up the quarterback's drop in the passing game and setting up pass protection as they were about presenting a credible threat of the run.

For Oregon, this is the second-straight drive that was killed because of a dropped pass on 3rd down.

Ohio State

Ohio State brought more pressure on this drive, which it doesn't look like Oregon was ready for. The 2nd & 9 field pressure put the defense in a great situation for 3rd & extra-long, allowing them to bring some unorthodox pressure without much threat of the run. Of course, they almost gave up a huge play, but got let off the hook when Oregon dropped a wide open pass.

Ohio State Drive 3 / Play 1 / 1ˢᵗ & 10 / +46 Yard Line / Left Hash / 2:35 1Q
Oregon 7 – OSU 7

Summary
Elliott runs for a gain of 6 yards.

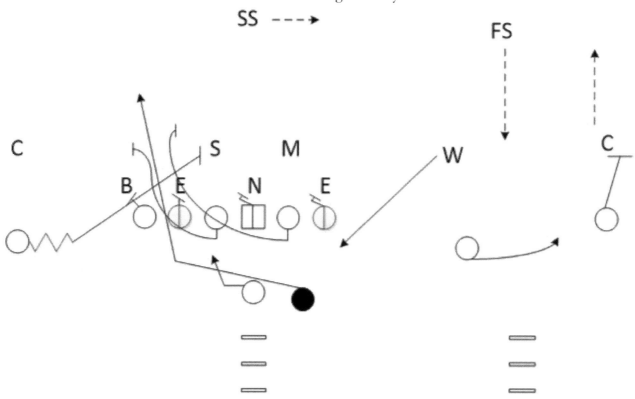

Analysis

The Buckeyes continue to use gap schemes, and now add an extra blocker at the point of attack by using the receiver to block down on an inside linebacker in order to create a crease off-tackle.

The Z is supposed to crack back on the 1st inside linebacker he sees, but in reality he doesn't block a soul. The corner to the playside does a great job of crack-replace technique by staying outside and playing contain once the Z receiver goes inside the formation to block.

The play is designed to hit in the C gap inside of the tight end's block of the outside linebacker, as the tackle manages to turn the playside defensive end. The first guard kicks out the cornerback, but the Sam linebacker shoots the gap and holds up the backside guard, slowing down the timing of the play. Still, the back manages to build up enough momentum to pick up a gain of six yards and get the offense ahead of the count on first down.

Ohio State Drive 3 / Play 2 / 2nd & 4 / +40 Yard Line / Left Hash / 2:24 1Q
Oregon 0 – OSU 0

Summary
Pass complete to Thomas out wide for 7 yards and a first down.

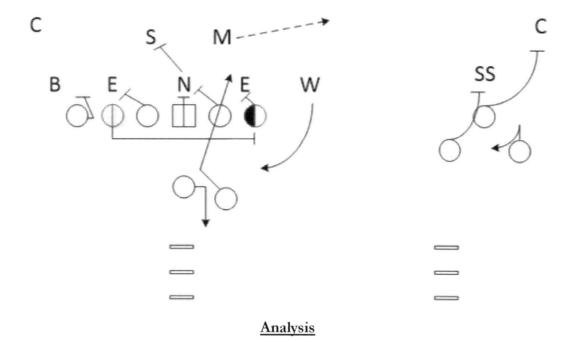

Analysis

Oregon gives a pre-snap look that makes throwing the hitch screen out to the bunch very attractive, since at first there are only two defenders aligned to that side of the formation. The particular pressure that the Duck defense brings is designed to get a third defender out wide, not to mention that the free safety chases the throw as well, giving the defense their coveted 4 on 3 advantage.

The hitch screen is packaged with a tackle-trap that is designed to create a running lane against just this sort of edge pressure. However the pre-snap numerical situation out on the edge cannot be ignored, and looks too attractive to pass up.

<u>Ohio State Drive 3 / Play 3 / 1st & 10 / +33 Yard Line / Right Hash / 1:56 1Q</u>
Oregon 7 – OSU 7
<u>Summary</u>

Defensive pass interference, automatic first down

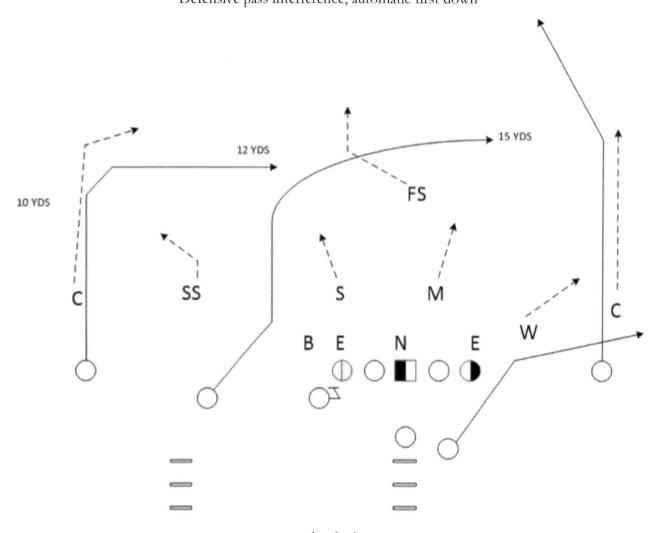

<u>Analysis</u>

The Oregon defense is in a simple cover 3 scheme, and the post-cross-dig concept is perfectly designed to attack this scheme.

The great thing about Urban Meyer's offense is the ability to use playaction with only the quarterback lined up in the backfield. Ohio State has completely flipped the field, and now Meyer wants to take a shot at the end zone. It looks like Cardale is waiting for the crossing route to come open, and when that doesn't happen, he throws the deep post, but it's too late, the window has closed.

<u>Ohio State Drive 3 / Play 4 / 1st & 10 / +18 Yard Line / Right Hash / 1:27 1Q</u>
Oregon 7 – OSU 7
<u>Summary</u>
Elliott run for a gain of 17 yards and a first down.

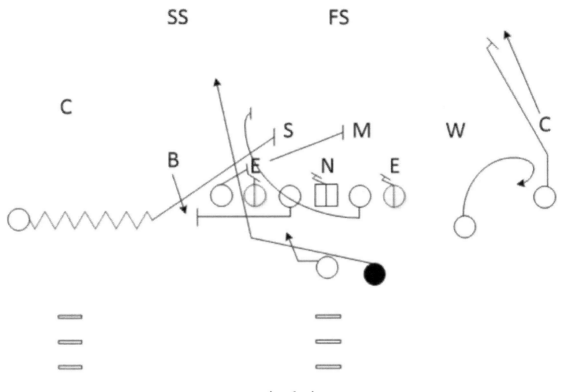

<u>Analysis</u>

The wide alignment of the outside linebacker to the field makes this an easy block for the pulling guard. Normally the tight end would block out on the outside backer to his side, but since he is aligned so far wide, the tight end works in conjunction with the left tackle to combo back to the Mike linebacker, which seals him off from making a play and chasing the ball carrier down from the backside.

The Z receiver coming in short motion seals off the front side linebacker, and creates a huge running lane to the field that nearly gets the back into the end zone.

This time instead of running the pin and pull scheme to the short side of the field, they flip the strength of the formation and create a crease to the wide side of the field.

<u>Ohio State Drive 3 / Play 4 / 1st & Goal / +2 Yard Line / Left Hash / 1:18 1Q</u>
Oregon 7 – OSU 7
<u>Summary</u>
Touchdown! Pass complete to Nick Vannett from Cardale Jones.

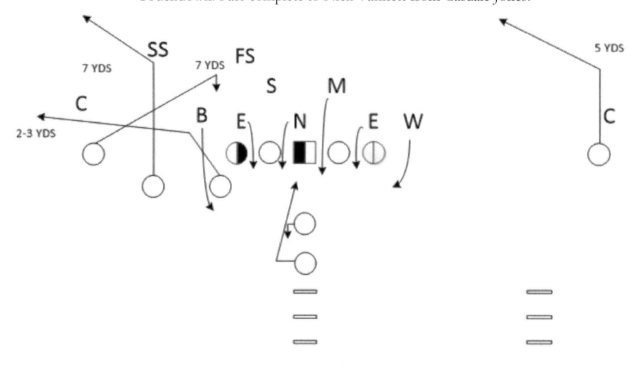

<u>Analysis</u>

This is a perfect example of creating "bunch" scenarios using non-bunch formations. It's an easy read and a very simple concept. The playfake, along with the with the Z receiver coming in from the outside creates a rub that frees up the flat route. The small amount of space behind the defense on the goal line limits the number of complex coverages that Oregon can play, and as such they are limited to simple man coverage.

Cardale delays a bit in getting the ball out to the flat as quickly as he probably could have, but he gets it to the tight end in time, and it's another touchdown for Ohio State.

With all the pressure brought from Oregon, it should be noted that the backside receiver is one-on-one with the defensive back, and not even having an underneath defender to that side who can threaten to undercut the route. The receiver has inside leverage on the corner and can roam free on the slant route to that half of the field.

OREGON FIELD GOAL BLOCK

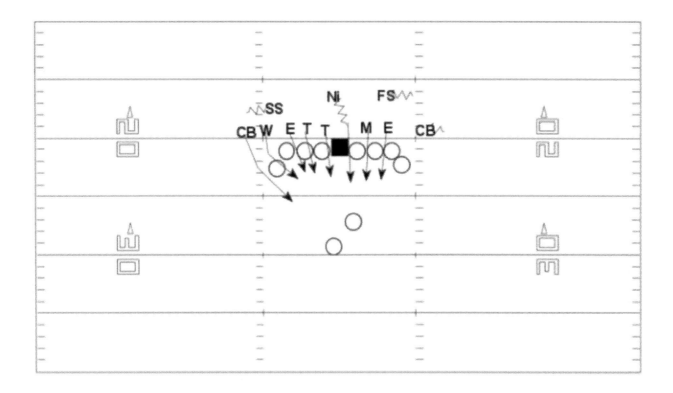

Ohio State Drive #3 Review

<u>Ohio State</u>

Once again the offense forces the defense to account for the run-adjust passes on the opposite side of the formation, as well as attacking off-tackle with the run game.

<u>Oregon</u>

The defense has made a habit out of bringing edge pressure from the field, and even which forced the offense to attack the wide side of the field with a hitch screen.

Ohio State is getting into a groove on offense, and getting more and more comfortable with what Oregon is doing defensively, so the Ducks need to be a little bit more unexpected with their pressures and coverages, otherwise the Buckeyes are in danger of running away with this game.

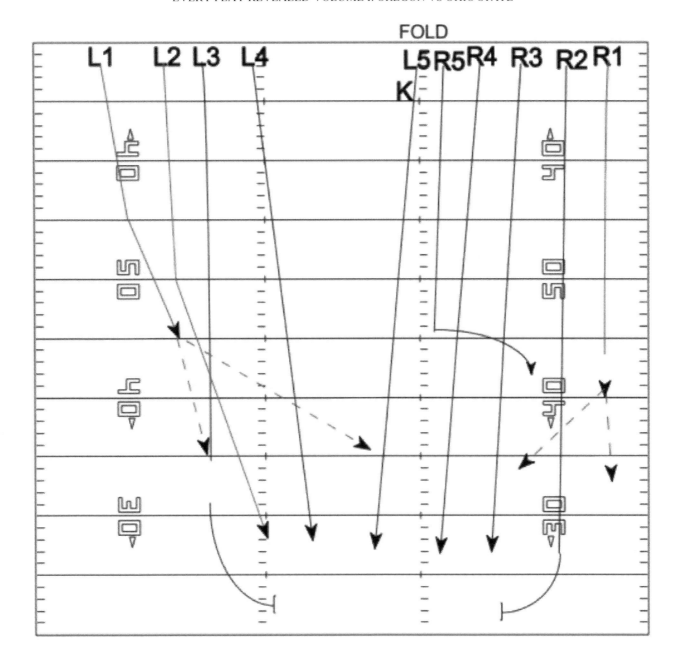

Analysis

This is the same idea as the last Ohio State kickoff as they're trying to get the football to the alley outside of the right hash.

OREGON

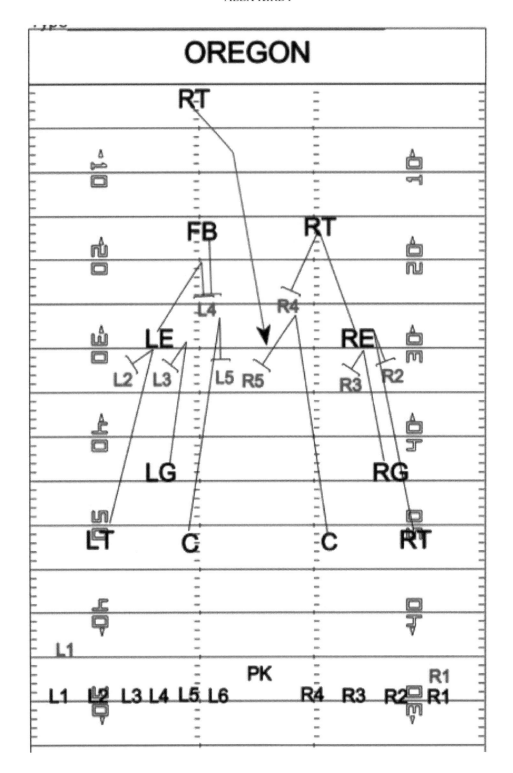

<u>Oregon Drive 4 / Play 1 / 1st & 10 / -25 Yard Line / Left Hash / 1:08 1Q</u>
Oregon 7 – OSU 14
Summary
Travis Tyner run for a gain of 11 yards and a first down.

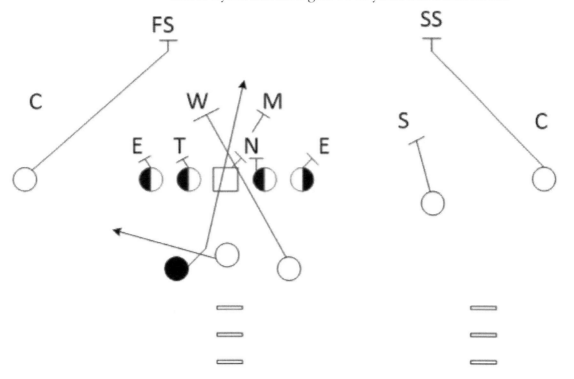

This is a big play for Oregon in this instance, a variation of the classic isolation play where the backs will cross, and add a bit of misdirection to what is normally a simple downhill run. The offensive line will block out on the down linemen in both directions, and the lead back will block the inside backer on the opposite side of the formation, while the center and the right guard will combo up to the Mike linebacker.

After starting slowly the previous couple of drives, Mark Helfrich wanted to get ahead of the count on first down and get things moving in a positive direction.

Oregon Drive 4 / Play 2 / 1st & 10 / -36 Yard Line / Left Hash / 1:02 1Q
Oregon 7 – OSU 14
Summary
Mariota runs for 7 yards.

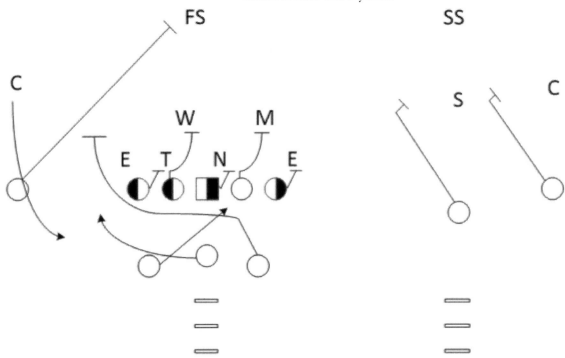

The defense comes on a corner blitz from the boundary, and the offense is running the zone read with the backside back coming from the other side to handle the scraper to the quarterback. The defensive line slants inside to account for the extra rush coming from the corner, which makes the quarterback's read that much easier.

When you get a corner free against this quarterback one-on-one on the blitz, it comes down to who the better athlete is, and in this case, that's Mariota. He makes a move then gets to the sideline for a decent gain on first down.

This is the second time Ohio State has brought the corner from the boundary, something they love to do, so it'll be interesting to watch if they stick with it against two-back formations as a way to disrupt the run game for Oregon.

Oregon Drive 4 / Play 3 / 2nd & 3 / -43 Yard Line / Left Hash / 0:51 1Q
Oregon 7 – OSU 14

Summary
Freeman runs for a gain of 2 yards

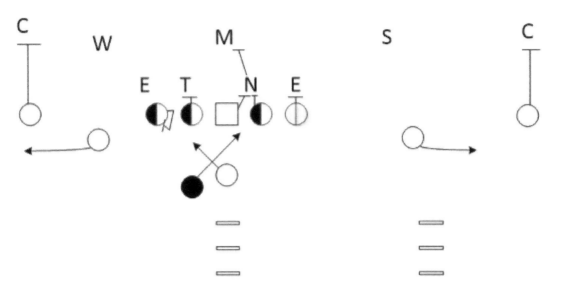

Analysis

After some success early on in the drive, Oregon goes back to their one-back inside zone.

The defense does exactly what it's designed to do by forcing the ball to bounce outside to an unblocked Sam linebacker who along with the Mike and the defensive end to that side helps bring the ball carrier down.

The back makes the right call since the three technique to that side squeezes the left guard and eliminated any hole that would've developed to the left side of the offensive line.

Oregon Drive 4 / Play 4 / 3rd & 6 / -40 Yard Line / Middle / 0:24 1Q

Oregon 7 – OSU 14

Summary

Incomplete pass

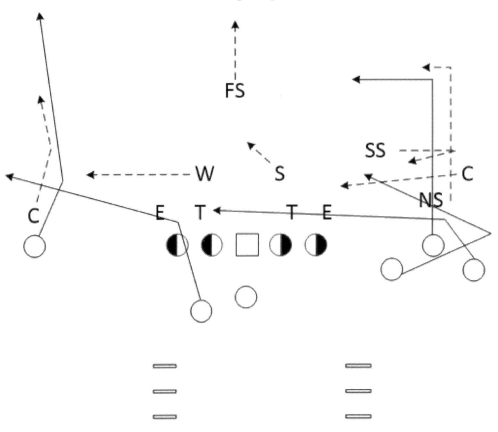

Analysis

This is a staple of most pro-style passing offenses in college and at the professional level, often referred to as the "jerk" route by the #3 receiver in the bunch. It starts with a traditional drive concept, a shallow cross with a basic cross coming in behind it, but instead of the #3 receiver heading out to the flat, he'll pivot back to the middle of the field and follow the drive route by the Z receiver, further flooding the middle of the field.

Mariota first looks to the flat route coming from the backfield, and once that's covered his eyes move from left to right, next to the drive, then to the basic cross coming in behind it, then to the jerk route coming in behind it.

The strong safety lined up over the bunch and tasked with covering the #3 receiver makes a heck of a play to knock the ball away from the receiver and force a punt.

2 MAN SHIELD LT

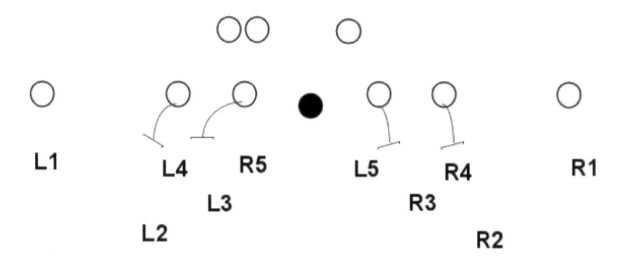

L1 **L4** **R5** **L5** **R4** **R1**

L3 **R3**

L2 **R2**

<u>Analysis</u>

- The punt team false starts on their first attempt, since the snapper forgets the snap count.

- The punt protection slides to the side of the pressure, the middle shield player should make that call whether the front line is sliding to the left or the right.

7 MAN
BLOCK

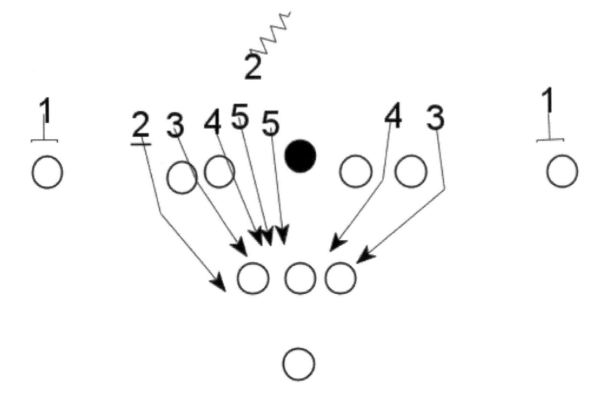

Oregon Drive #4 Review

Oregon

Oregon needs to find an answer for 3rd down. This is the third straight drive that ended on a catchable ball landing incomplete. It wasn't a drop in the most literal sense of the word, but the route could've been run a bit better, and the receiver could've gone after it a bit more. The Ducks are definitely feeling the lack of receiver depth in this game due to injuries and suspensions.

Still, there were some positives on this drive with the success they had running the ball out of two-back sets. They need to get back to that.

Ohio State

The defense needs to find an answer for the two-back run game, because Oregon can do some damage against this defensive front if they decide to add an extra blocker into the backfield. OSU's defense is pretty safe against most of the one-back stuff they do, but the Buckeyes need to have some more answers ready for the two-back looks, even if it's just an extra couple of blitzes that complement the corner blitz, from the boundary.

Ohio State Drive 4 / Play 1 / 1ˢᵗ & 10 / -37 Yard Line / Left Hash / 0:09 1Q
Oregon 7 – OSU 14
Summary
Elliott run for a gain of 1 yard

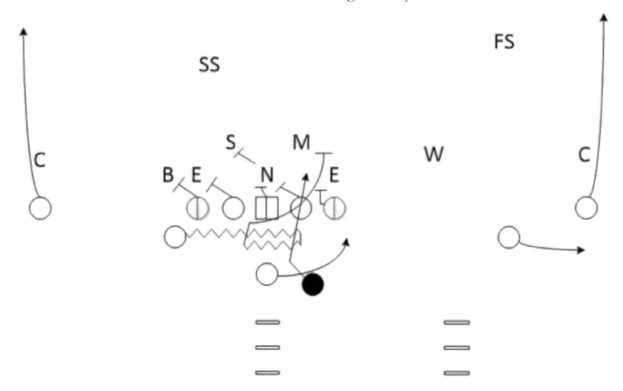

Analysis

This is referred to as an inside zone "search" play, which gives the zone scheme more of a downhill feel.

It's a very tough block for the left guard on the defensive end because of the wide splits on the offensive line, which in turn gives the defensive end more space to operate in. The right tackle gets beat inside by the defensive end over him.

The tight end off the ball and put in motion has the job to "search" the inside of the offensive line and find the running lane ahead of the tailback. He has the same reads as the tailback in the zone scheme, and gives the offense at the point of attack.

Ohio State Drive 4 / Play 2 / 2nd & 9 / -38 Yard Line / Left Hash / 15:00 2Q
Oregon 7 – OSU 14
Summary
Incomplete pass

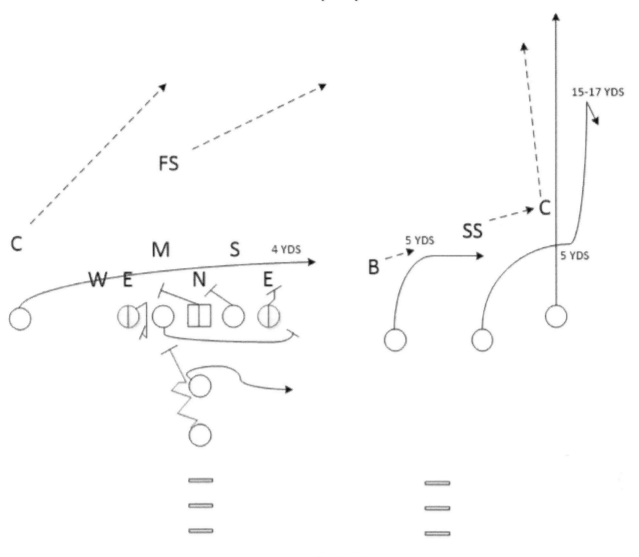

Analysis

Ohio State runs the same concept out of their trips formation with Cardale getting out to the edge. Oregon doesn't bring any edge pressure this time, and the quarterback's progression runs flat route, to the comeback, to the shallow crossing route coming from the other side.

This would've been an easy completion but the tight end was knocked off his route by the outside linebacker. It looks like the defense is experimenting with whether or not to bring the outside linebacker to the strong side.

Ohio State Drive 4 / Play 3 / 3rd & 9 / -38 Yard Line / Left Hash / 14:53 2Q
Oregon 7 – OSU 14
Summary
Cardale Jones scrambles for 17 yards and a first down.

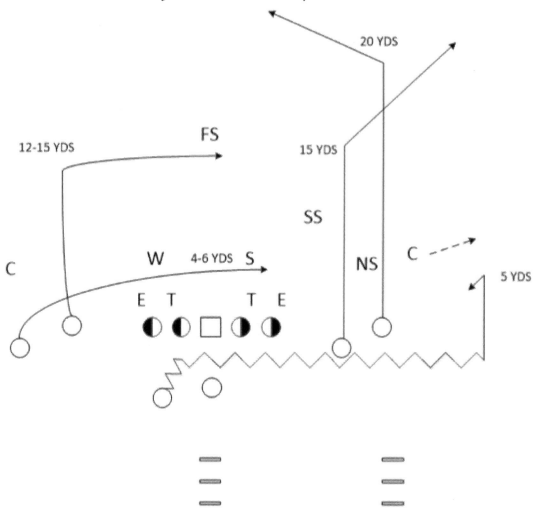

Analysis

The reason the offense motions the running back out wide is to take the corner out of the equation and open up the area on the field deep. The #3 receiver running the corner route at fifteen yards should find a vacant area behind him. Still, Cardale is focused on the drive concept to the left side of the field.

The pass rush does not give Cardale enough time to wait for the route to come open but he finds running room down the left sideline and picks up the first down.

It's all about keeping the reads simple in the passing game, and by spreading out the defenders it makes it tougher for the defense to disguise their intentions.

Ohio State Drive 4 / Play 4 / 1ˢᵗ & 10 / +45 Yard Line / Left Hash / 14:46 2Q
Oregon 7 – OSU 14
Summary
Pass complete for a 6 yard gain

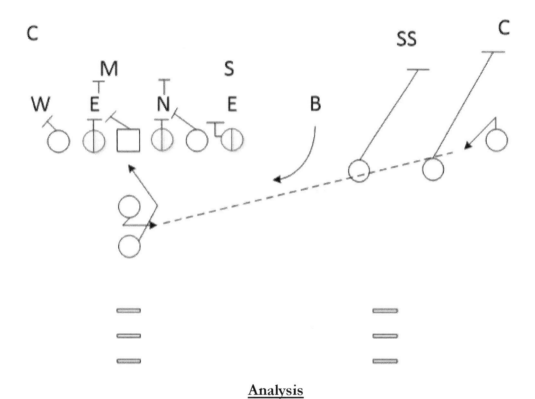

Analysis

The strong outside linebacker is threatening pre-snap, so Cardale gets direction from the sideline to carry out the play fake and get the ball out on the edge. The edge pressure from the (B) is trying to get into the path of the ball being thrown to the hitch screen out wide. The receiver manages to pick up five yards on first down, even with the poor blocking out on the edge by the other receivers.

Throwing the hitch route is something that Ohio State does well, and it's worth noting that even with subpar blocking out on the edge by the receivers it's usually been successful, since it's more important for those guys to just get in the way and allow the receiver to make moves in the open.

Ohio State Drive 4 / Play 5 / 2nd & 4 / +39 Yard Line / Right Hash / 14:11 2Q
Oregon 7 – OSU 14
Summary
Fumble at the mesh point and recovered by Oregon

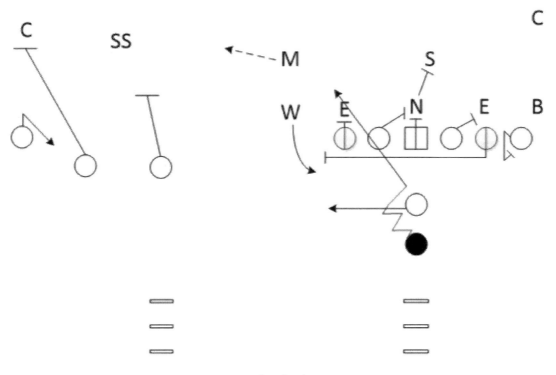

Analysis

A screwup at the mesh point causes a fumble and a turnover in the backfield.

If they had managed to block the play correctly, this is undoubtedly going for a big gain, since the tackle kicks out one side of the running lane, then the left guard comes off of the combo block and seals off the Sam linebacker as well.

Ohio State Drive #4 Review

<u>Ohio State</u>

The Buckeyes are continuing to mix up the run game and bring out new schemes, including the inside zone search concept, while at the same time, making the defense account for run-adjust throws to the wide of the field. They're marching the ball down the field until the mix-up in the backfield that creates the fumble.

Still, there is a lot to take away from this drive.

<u>Oregon</u>

The Ducks are becoming more and more consistent with the amount of pressure they're bringing off the edge, especially against 3x1 formations. They're lucky to get out of this drive without giving up any points.

Oregon Drive 5 / Play 1 / 1st & 10 / -41 Yard Line / Left Hash / 13:49 2Q
Oregon 7 – OSU 14

Summary
Pass complete to Baylis for 7 yards

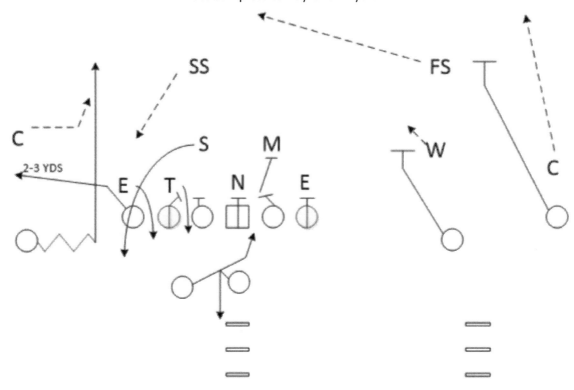

Analysis

Mariota is going to throw the flat route almost every time unless he's given a really good reason not to. Oregon brings the Z receiver in short motion to a tighter split, where to the defense it appears as if he's going to "crack-back" block on the near inside linebacker. The defense reacts to the short split into the boundary by bringing edge pressure with the defensive line toward the back slanting inside.

It's a way to disguise the fact that they're doing the same thing again, throwing the flat route and springing him open to the short side of the field.

Oregon Drive 5 / Play 2 / 2nd & 3 / -48 Yard Line / Left Hash / 13:43 2Q
Oregon 7 – OSU 14
Summary

Tyner runs for a gain of 4 yards and a 1st down.

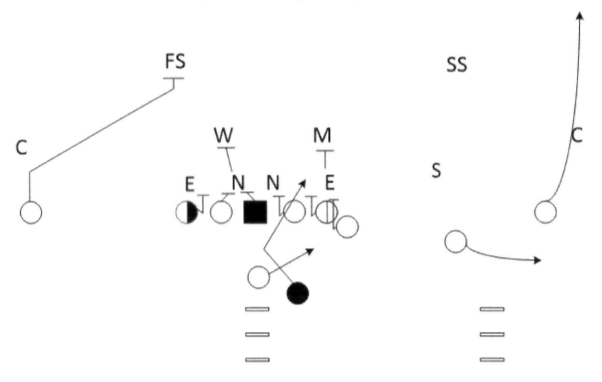

Analysis

A designed cutback run, especially with the two defensive tackles shaded on the center at the same time, there's not much room on the front side. The TE off the line of scrimmage works in tandem with the right tackle to seal off the defensive end and the scraping Mike linebacker on the backside. The Sam comes off his defense of the bubble route and makes the tackle, but not before the offense picks up the first down.

Oregon is still committed to finding a reliable way to run the football in one-back formations, and they've had only mediocre success so far.

Oregon Drive 5 / Play 3 / 1st & 10 / +48 Yard Line / Left Hash / 13:31 2Q
Oregon 7 – OSU 14
Summary
Pass complete to Marshall for a gain of 20 yards and a first down

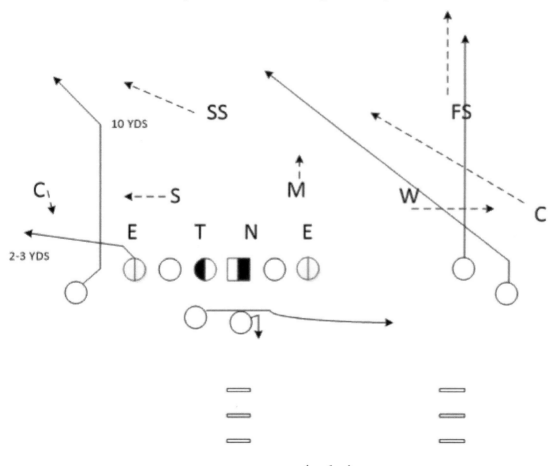

Analysis

This is another variation on the crossing route concept, where the smash side of the formation does the job of occupying the deep defenders to that side of the field instead of just running themselves out of the play. The angle of the crossing route coming from the backside means that he's basically running an elongated slant route, and can run the route while being ready to receive the pass at just about any time without losing momentum.

Oregon Drive 5 / Play 4 / 1st & 10 / +28 Yard Line / Left Hash / 13:00 2Q
Oregon 7 – OSU 14
Summary
Pass to Stanford for a 1 yard gain

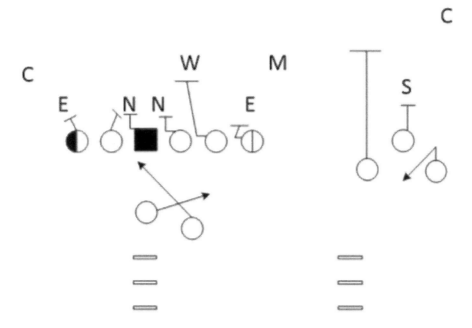

Analysis

The offense is trying to get the ball out on the edge in a hurry, but the Sam linebacker lined up over the point of the bunch beats the block, gets into the backfield, and ends up making the tackle on the hitch screen.

Once again, notice that the Sam linebacker isn't pressing the point of the bunch, which gives the defenders to that side of the formation room to maneuver in case of a quick pass to the wide side of the field.

<u>Oregon Drive 5 / Play 5 / 2nd & 9 / +27 Yard Line / Right Hash / 12:46 2Q</u>
Oregon 7 – OSU 14
<u>Summary</u>
Pass complete to Stanford for 17 yards.

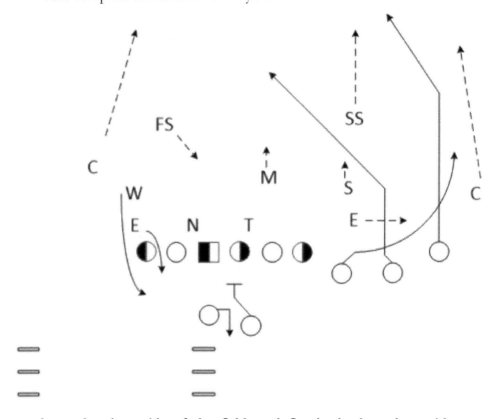

Oregon continues their assault on the short side of the field, and floods the boundary with more receivers than Ohio State has defenders.

The only flat defender is the defensive end, and he falls to the ground after trying to disrupt the post route of #2, meaning that there is no underneath defender to the boundary who is able to get underneath the wheel route, making it a pretty easy catch and throw for Oregon.

This is a great way to win the numbers game downfield, as well as force the defense to account for the vertical passing game out of unbalanced sets.

Oregon Drive 5 / Play 6 / 1st & Goal / +10 Yard Line / Right Hash / 12:32 2Q
Oregon 7 – OSU 14

Summary
Pass complete to Baylis for 3 yards.

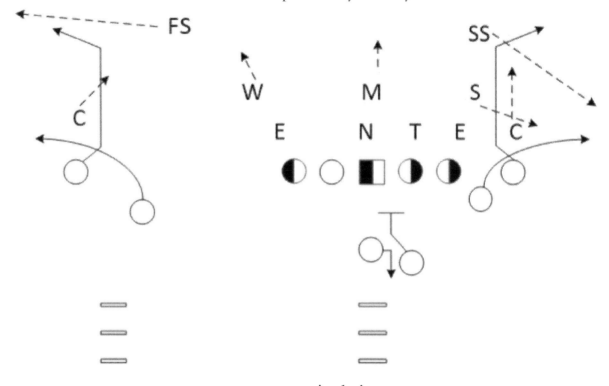

Analysis

Oregon uses Ohio State's defensive scheme against them by creating a rub on the inside defenders using the #1 receiver. He walls off the inside linebacker and safety, and the tight end runs to the flat wide open for an easy completion.

This concept has been one of the most consistent themes in the first half for Oregon, attacking the flats to short side of the field and creating rubs on defenders using stacked receiver sets.

Oregon Drive 5 / Play 7 / 2nd & Goal / +7 Yard Line / Right Hash / 12:14 2Q
Oregon 7 – OSU 14
Summary
Incomplete pass

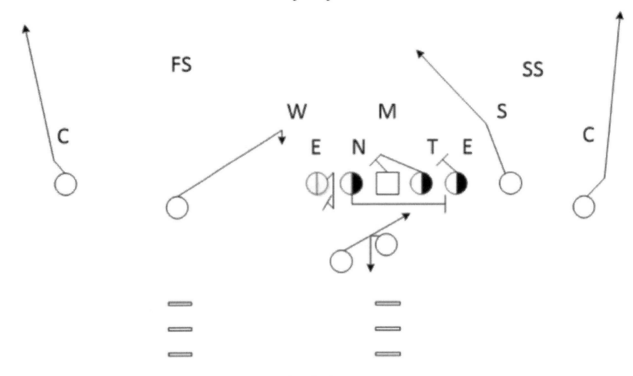

Analysis

I like the idea behind this play, but I'm not a fan of exactly how it's designed. The route by the slot receiver brings the free safety closer to the middle of the field, and as a result the window between the two safeties is much smaller than it could've been. Mariota has to put the ball up high where only his tight end could get the ball, but even he can't grab the pass.

The pulling guard really helps sell this to the defenders up front, and clears the way for the tight end to come over the top of the linebacker without encountering too much resistance.

<u>Oregon Drive 5 / Play 8 / 3rd & Goal / +7 Yard Line / Right Hash / 11:43 2Q</u>
Oregon 7 – OSU 14
<u>Summary</u>
Mariota runs for 4 yards.

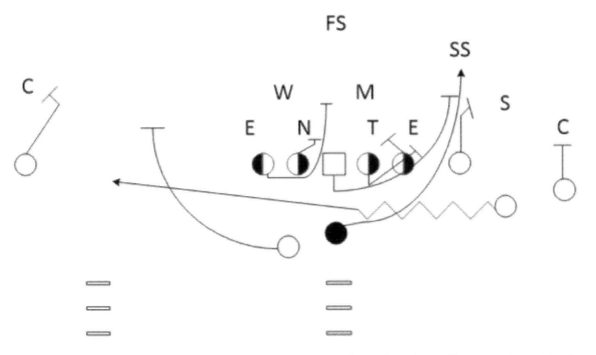

The front side defensive end comes up the field, disrupting the pulling guard and forcing the play out wide where the members of the secondary can make the tackle.

The offense is asking the right guard to complete a very tough assignment by asking him to get his head across the defensive end when it's likely that he'll be playing up the field like that by virtue of his pre-snap alignment.

The play is designed to hit up inside the tight end's slightly flexed alignment, but the defensive end does a great job of spilling the play outside where the corner and safety can make a play.

Oregon Drive 5 / Play 9 / 4th & Goal / +3 Yard Line / Right Hash / 11:36 2Q
Oregon 7 – OSU 14

Summary

Turnover on downs. Tyner runs for 2 yards and is stopped short of the goal line.

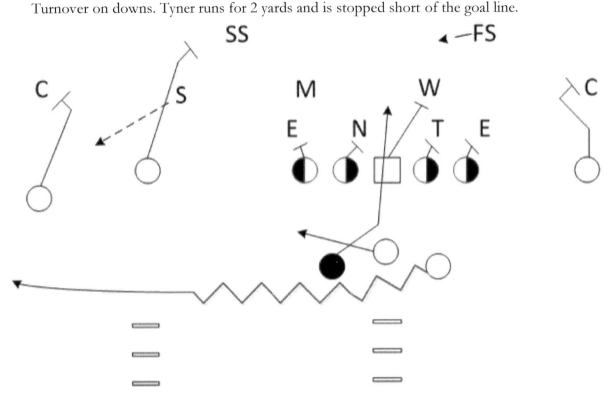

The motion doesn't remove anyone from the box, and with the offense being so close to the goal line, the free safety also comes down into the gap, who along with the Mike linebacker stops the back short of the goal line. If the left guard had been able to turn the defensive tackle outside, the back could cut back to the backside of the formation and it's an easy score. As it stands, the back did exactly what he was supposed to do, but the defense had a numbers advantage at the point of attack.

If the defense isn't removing anyone from the box, you're putting yourself at a huge disadvantage. It's also important to note that Oregon had not run this formation and motion combination early on in the game, so they were basically just guessing as to how the defense would react without any real evidence from this game to go off of.

I actually love the decision to go for the score here, since Oregon get to this point by not playing scared. It would be pretty ridiculous to change your thought process in the biggest game of the year, and it would send a message to your team that you're changing who you are. Now if you want to criticize the play call here, I can understand that.

Oregon Drive #5 Review

Oregon

A lot of this drive was spent experimenting with different formations and schemes to find a way to consistently move the football using one-back formations.

They haven't given the defense much to worry about with all the hitch and bubble screens packaged with inside zone schemes. That probably has a lot to do with how difficult it's been to run off-tackle so far, since every attempt to run in the C gap has been spilled to the outside.

4TH DOWN PLAY—If you're calling the play, run an Iso and it's a TD. The motion didn't really remove anyone from the box, and there's also the safety to worry about since it's so close to the goal line. The two guys who aren't accounted for in the blocking scheme are the two guys who make the tackle.

Ohio State

The Buckeye defense has begun to clamp down even more on the interior of the offensive line, twice covering up the center on both sides with two defensive tackles making it tough for the center to work on double team blocks. Whichever the direction the center ends up moving to block, the defensive tackle to the opposite side will shoot through the gap and try to disrupt the run game in the backfield.

Ohio State Drive 5 / Play 1 / 1st & 10 / -1 Yard Line / Left Hash / 11:10 2Q
Oregon 7 – OSU 14

Summary
Cardale Jones runs for 1 yard on the QB sneak.

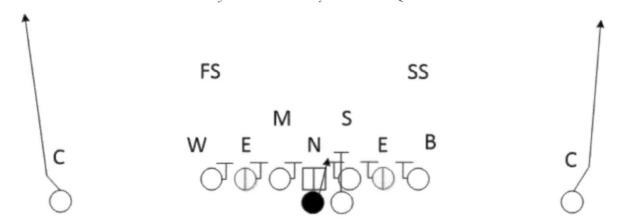

Analysis

The safeties are at a depth of six yards, and the linebackers are up near the line of scrimmage. Meanwhile the offensive line has almost no space in between each guy to minimize the threat of penetration.

The offense is just trying to get out of the shadow of their own goal line, but they're only able to pick up one yard.

Ohio State Drive 5 / Play 2 / 2nd & 9 / -2 Yard Line / Left Hash / 10:59 2Q
Oregon 7 – OSU 14
Summary

Elliott runs for a gain of 26 yards and a first down

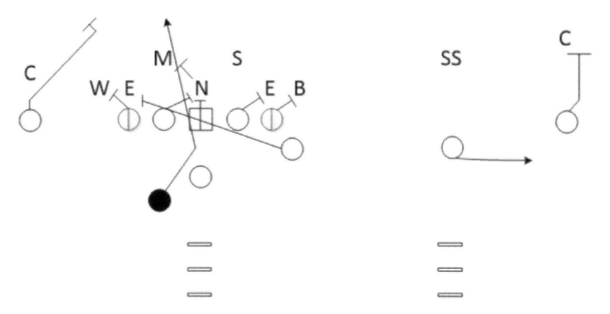

Analysis

This time the nose tackle is lined up head up on the center, so the next widest down lineman is the defensive end lined up over the left tackle. At the same time, trapping the defensive end means that the offense can't put a body on the backside inside linebacker, but at the same time, he tries to come over the top when he sees the tight end cross the formation to put a block on the defensive lineman. As a result, when the front side running lane is clogged up, there is all kinds of room on the backside because the inside linebacker over pursued the play.

This is exactly what happens on the play, where the back stays patient, doesn't panic, and ends up with a big gain because the defense played unsound and undisciplined.

Ohio State Drive 5 / Play 3 / 1ˢᵗ & 10 / -28 Yard Line / Left Hash / 10:19 2Q
Oregon 7 – OSU 14
Summary
Completion to Vannett for a gain of 8 yards

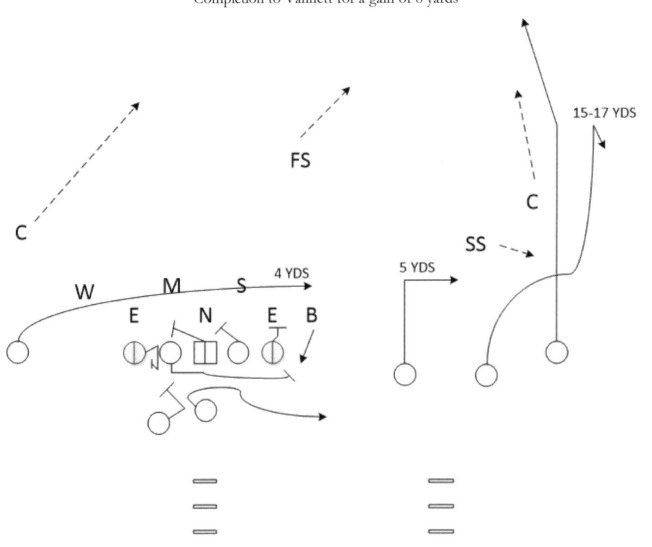

Analysis

Ohio State once again running this boot concept that's worked well for them a couple of times earlier in the game. The edge pressure keeps Cardale hemmed in but he manages to get the ball out to the tight end in bounds.

The defense doesn't even try to disguise their intentions, showing the edge pressure from the B position and the Sam walks out to split the difference between the offensive tackle and the #3 receiver.

It's practically a race to the edge because the #3 receiver has a head start on the inside linebacker creeping out in coverage.

Ohio State Drive 5 / Play 4 / 2nd & 2 / -36 Yard Line / Right Hash / 9:47 2Q
Oregon 7 – OSU 14

Summary
Elliott runs for a 5 yard gain and a first down.

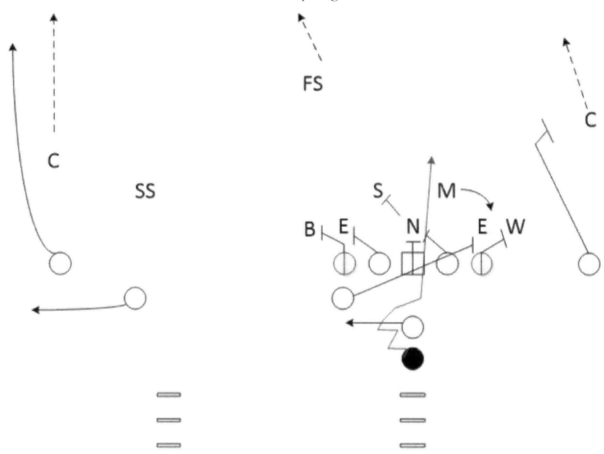

Analysis

Once again we see the defense bring pressure on the front side of the play and forcing the cutback. The back finds a hole in the backside A gap that is quickly closed down by the defensive end coming across the face of the left guard but only after the offense picks up the first down.

The linebacker blitz opposite the tight end off the line of scrimmage is a way to attack the wham play. Seeing the tight end off the line is an alert for the defense that he's likely to come right back across the formation for a wham play like they've already ran several times tonight.

Ohio State Drive 5 / Play 5 / 1ˢᵗ & 10 / -41 Yard Line / Right Hash / 9:22 2Q
Oregon 7 – OSU 14

Summary
Pass completed to Smith for a gain of 50 yards and fumbled, recovered by Oregon

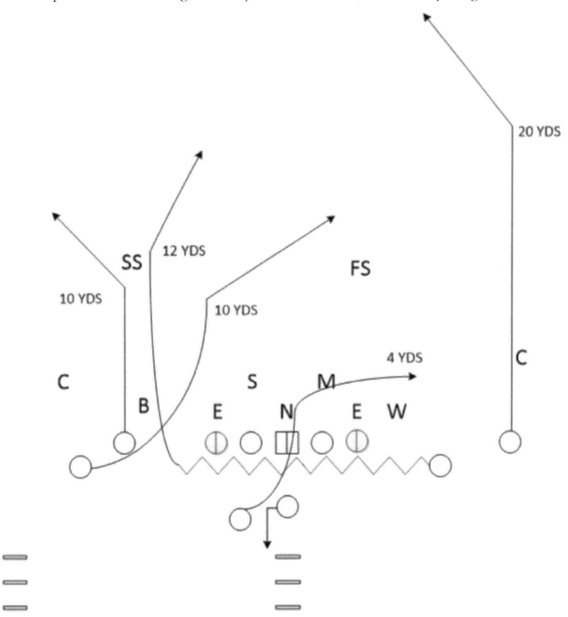

This pass play hits exactly where it's designed to, about 25 yards down the field outside of the right hash, in a vacant area where the X receiver cleared out the corner to that side of the field on the post route. This would have been a tremendous play for the Buckeyes, but the receiver is stripped when the corner puts his helmet on the football and pops it out for the Ducks to recover.

Ohio State Drive #5 Review

Ohio State

Once again, a simple and avoidable mistake kills a very promising drive for Ohio State and keeps Oregon in the football game. Not long after 98 yard drive, Ohio State was a lost fumble away from taking another drive the length of the field.

Oregon

The first big play of the drive is a wham play that the ball carrier cuts back when the backside defensive end and linebacker come over the top and leave their assigned gaps. This defense needs to play with better fits. They got very lucky on the strip and fumble down the field, because right now the only thing stopping Ohio State is Ohio State.

Oregon Drive 6 / Play 1 / 1ˢᵗ & 10 / -9 Yard Line / Left Hash / 8:46 2Q
Oregon 7 – OSU 14
Summary
Freeman runs for a gain of 3 yards.

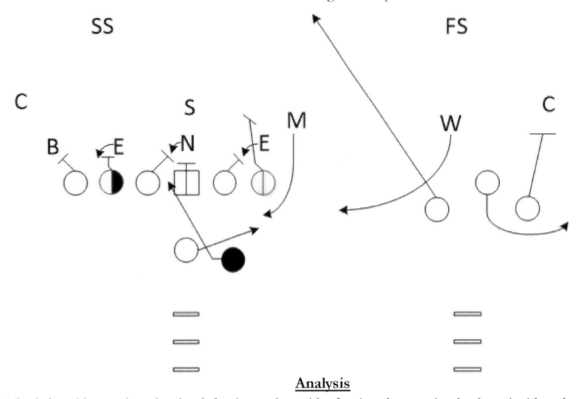

Analysis

The left tackle gets beat by the defensive end outside, forcing the running back up inside, where the Sam linebacker is waiting because the left guard hasn't come off the combo block on the nose, as a result he's completely unblocked and able to make the tackle, but not until the offense picks up four yards.

The offensive line has been coached up on the sideline in between drives to recognize the current look from the defense as a blitz key. A stand up 9 technique outside of the tight end combined with a 4i technique with the defensive end on the inside shoulder of the left tackle tells the offensive line that the exact same field pressure is coming from the weak side of the formation as they got the last time.

As a result, the offense runs an inside zone scheme, which allows them to double team the nose, and the right tackle can work with the right guard to secure the backside gaps while climbing to the second level. It's a brilliant job of coaching by the coaches and recognition by the guys up front to make the proper adjustments.

Oregon Drive 6 / Play 2 / 2ⁿᵈ & 6 / -13 Yard Line / Left Hash / 8:36 2Q
Oregon 7 – OSU 14

Summary

Freeman runs for a gain of 2 yards

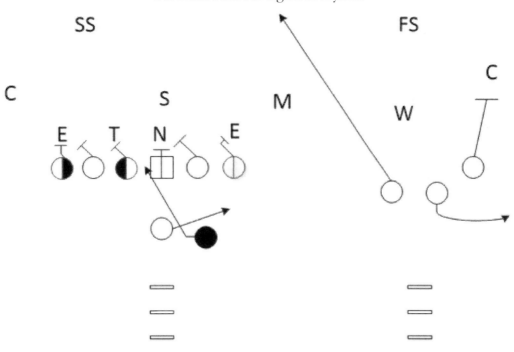

Analysis

The offense lines back up in a hurry and runs the same play, with the only noticeable change being that the #2 receiver and the #3 receiver switch places on the line of scrimmage before the snap. The weak side defensive end beats the right tackle inside, and collapses on the running back that had originally hit the B gap where the running lane suddenly disappeared when the defensive end beats the right tackle.

On this play, it's a normal, base-defense look from the four down linemen on defense, which actually ends up working against the offense. The right guard, instead of working with the right tackle to help on the defensive end, blocks down on the nose tackle along with the center.

<u>Oregon Drive 6 / Play 3 / 3rd & 5 / -14 Yard Line / Left Hash / 8:14 2Q</u>
Oregon 7 – OSU 14
<u>Summary</u>
Sack! Mariota sacked for a loss of 5 yards.

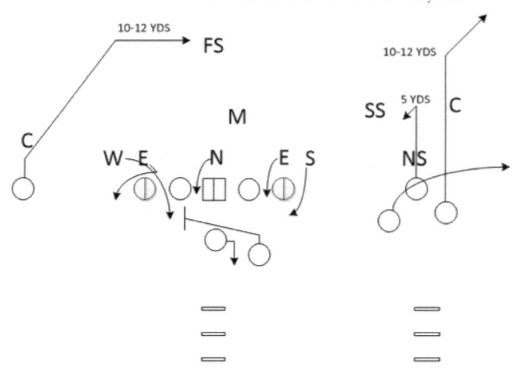

<u>Analysis</u>

This is another variation on the bunch routes, and Oregon is looking for answers on how to throw a pass out of the alignment against this particular brand of bunch coverage from Ohio State.

This play is totally designed to get the ball out to the flat to the #3 receiver. The point man on the bunch gets beat up by the nickel safety off the line of scrimmage, and the #1 receiver runs corner route which also serves to wall off any inside defenders, leaving the flat route wide open. Mariota is looking for the flat route but the pressure in his face forces him to step up and he's eventually sacked before he can get rid of the football.

You can also look at this as a variation of the rub routes that Oregon ran to the boundary all game.

OREGON PUNT FORMATIONS

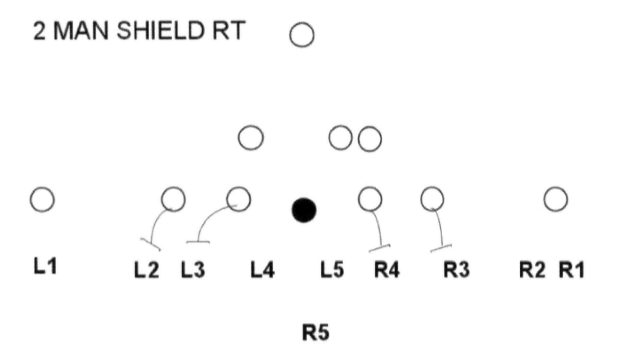

Analysis

Oregon is backed up in a scary spot, but they're not close enough to their own end zone to play a tight punt formation, since there is more than 14 yards from the line of scrimmage to the back of the end zone, so Oregon doesn't have to line up in tight splits. They're less worried about ball placement down the field than they are about getting the ball off on time.

OHIO STATE PUNT RETURN FORMATIONS

8 MAN BLOCK

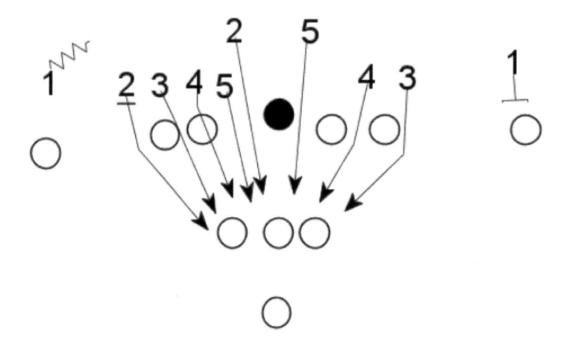

Oregon Drive #6 Review

Oregon

The Ducks stay committed to running the football out of one-back looks, this time trying the 3x1 formation with a tight end as the single receiver side away from the three receivers to the wide side of the field. Even with a tight end, it's still tough to get movement on the front side while protecting the backside and preventing penetration on the other side of the offensive line.

Ohio State

At the moment, Ohio State isn't concerned one bit with Mariota throwing the bubble routes or hitch screens off of a run action.

It looks like in many instances that Ohio State may be better off just playing base defenses and not sending pressures. Their defensive linemen are quick enough to chase down the play from behind, and get the jump off the snap on the line of scrimmage.

Ohio State Drive 6 / Play 1 / 1st & 10 / +49 Yard Line / Middle / 7:05 2Q
Oregon 7 – OSU 14
Summary
Incomplete pass

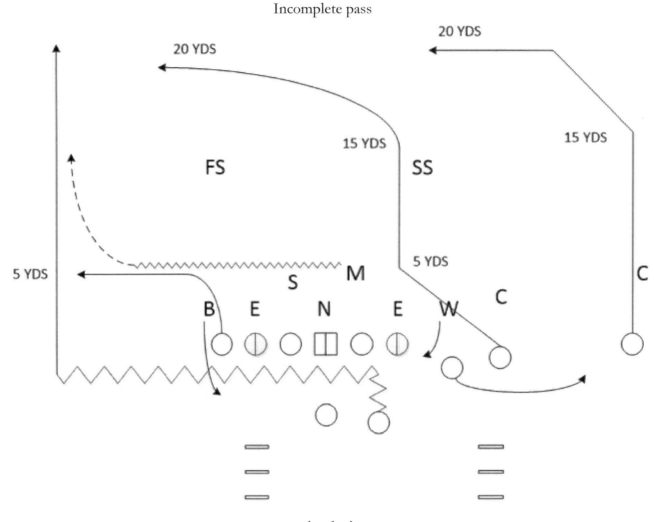

Analysis

The pass rush flushes Cardale from the pocket to the right, where there are no receivers in a good positions to catch an outlet pass. He's never ever in a good position to set his feet and throw an accurate pass. He manages to throw the ball out of bounds.

Defense goes "corners-over," which should set off alarm bells. Cardale is waiting on the tight end out route to come open, but the bubble is wide open because of the safety covering it is so deep.

The Mike linebacker follows the back in motion out of the backfield because he has him locked up in man coverage.

Ohio State Drive 6 / Play 2 / 2nd & 10 / +49 Yard Line / Middle / 6:57 2Q
Oregon 7 – OSU 14

Summary
Marshall runs for a loss of 2 yards.

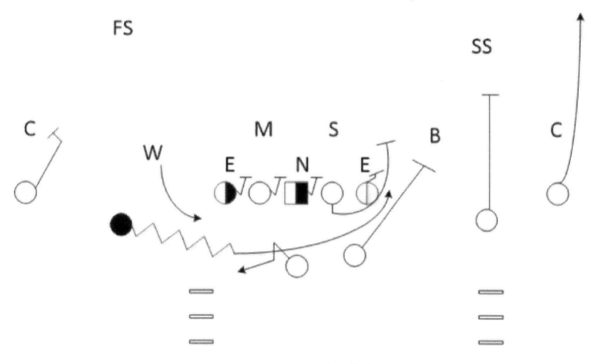

Analysis

This has been a great indicator of the run when the receiver comes in motion to receive the handoff in jet motion.

The right guard kicks out the blitzing B linebacker, who comes in so tight that he renders the blocking back invalid.

There's such a wall of defenders to the frontside of the play, and so much leakage on the backside, this play has practically no chance.

Ohio State Drive 6 / Play 3 / 3rd & 12 / -49 Yard Line / Right Hash / 6:45 2Q
Oregon 7 – OSU 14
Summary

Pass complete to Smith for a gain of 45 yards and a first down.

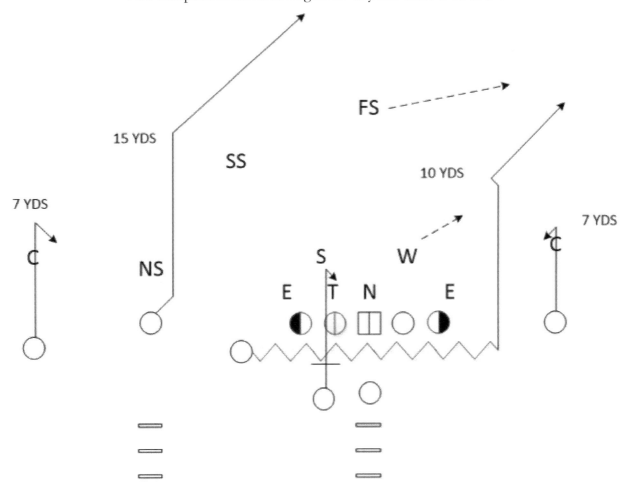

Analysis

Cardale's eyes stay outside of the right hash, so he reads low to high, sees the defense blanketing the short side of the field, then his eyes go to the backside post. He buys time with his feet, escapes the pocket, then gets the ball to an open receiver with only the strong safety trailing behind him in a Cover 2 deep half zone.

Ohio State is attacking the deep right side of the field again after the big play on the last drive.

Ohio State Drive 6 / Play 4 / +6 Yard Line / Right Hash / 6:06 2Q
Oregon 7 – OSU 14
Summary
Cardale Jones runs for 2 yards

Analysis

Against a wildcat formation like this, the Oregon defense puts two linebackers on the edge coming up the field to shut down any jet sweep, which is the staple of this formation, and the defense is selling out on stopping the perimeter run.

The path of the pulling guard's angle is too wide and the Mike linebacker comes in tight and shuts down the play.

Cardale's vision in the run game leaves a lot to be desired, and he appears to be coached up to not make more than a single cut when finding a running lane.

The offense is now lined up is basically a type of wildcat formation, only the quarterback is still taking the snap.

Ohio State Drive 6 / Play 5 / 2nd & Goal / +4 Yard Line / Middle / 5:31 2Q
Oregon 7 – OSU 14
Summary
Cardale Jones runs for a gain of 3 yards

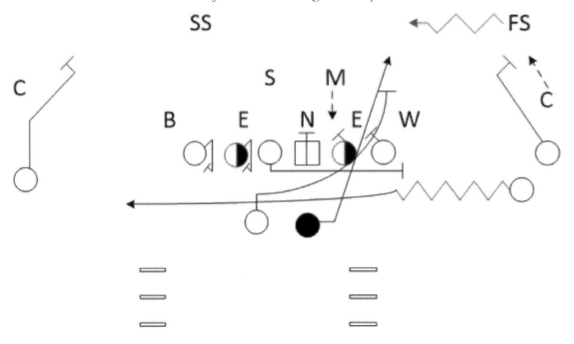

Analysis

The pulling guard kicks out the outside linebacker, but takes a poor angle, has no balance, and isn't able to sustain his block, and the outside linebacker ends up making the tackle.

The Mike blitzes into the A gap and makes it an easy block for the right guard, they seal off the gap.

The pulling guard needs to get his head inside of the outside linebacker to maintain leverage.

It's a quarterback counter play that packages the misdirection of a jet fake with the gap blocking and downhill running of a power play.

Ohio State Drive 6 / Play 6 / 3rd & Goal / +1 Yard Line / Right Hash / 4:55 2Q
Oregon 7 – OSU 14
Summary
Touchdown! Cardale Jones runs it in on the QB sneak for a 1 yard gain and a score!

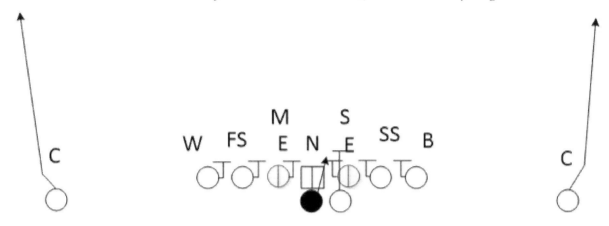

Analysis

The offensive line steps to their inside gap on the quarterback sneak, the back aligns in the strongside A gap and works as almost a lead back to provide that little extra push in this situation.

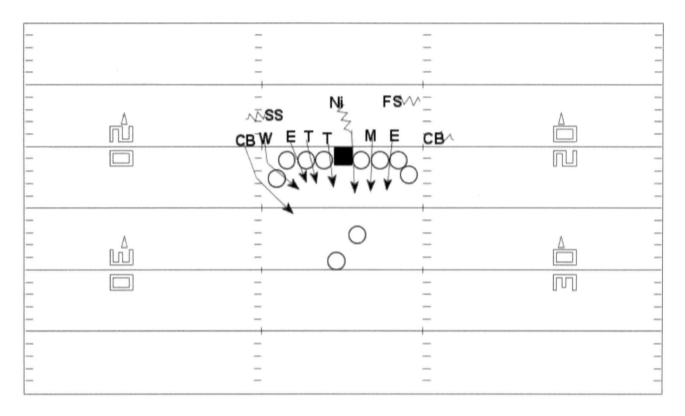

Analysis

The field goal block team comes off the edge, and the left wing should've been called for tripping the corner coming off the left side.

Ohio State Drive #6 Review

Ohio State

While Cardale had scrambled around for yardage a few times already, Ohio State goes the extra mile and calls two designed QB runs down near the goal line to finish the job.

Of particular interest is the quarterback counter, which was incredibly wide open to the backside, especially with the stacked receiver forcing the Will to widen.

Oregon

The defense is being gashed by gap schemes, but also has a habit of giving up big plays on 3rd and long, especially on the defensive deep left side.

They've been bringing pressure and getting Cardale off of his progression and flushed him from the pocket.

They've also made a habit of bracketing the short side of the field, meaning that they are effectively out-leveraging and out-numbering the offense into the boundary side of things, taking away the easy throws and forcing Cardale to go to his 3rd and 4th options. Unfortunately for Oregon, Cardale's 3rd option is wide open down the field.

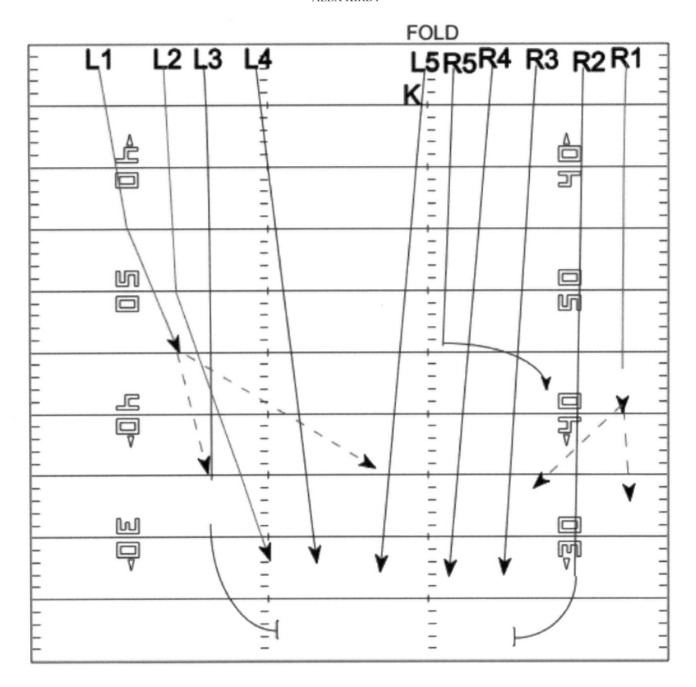

Analysis

The L1 and R1 have a responsibility to not get beat outside, since everyone else is busy forcing the ball inside.

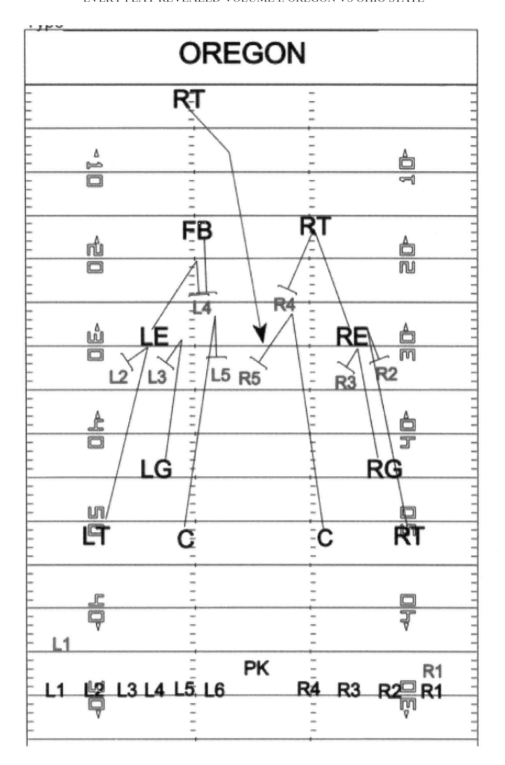

Oregon Drive 7 / Play 1 / 1st & 10 / -25 Yard Line / Middle / 4:49 2Q
Oregon 7 – OSU 21

Summary
Mariota gain of 2 yards on the keeper

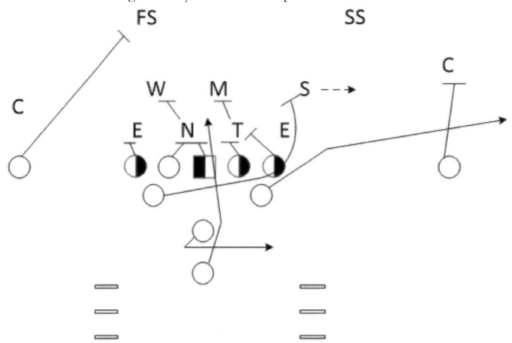

Analysis

The defense is playing cover 4 backside safety comes downhill on an angle to the opposite side of the formations when he sees #2 go across on the bluff path. The backside safety and Will linebacker are chasing the flow very aggressively, something Oregon could take advantage of.

Interesting path by the right tackle, ending up completely perpendicular to the LOS as if he's pulling but actually gains depth for his double team on the 3 tech.

#2 on the flat route peaks over his outside shoulder looking for a hot throw. Once he gets out to the numbers on his route, he'll look back inside to try to create a running lane for the QB in the alley.

Mariota is tackled by the backside safety, the guy who is unaccounted for in the blocking scheme.

After the last time when Oregon lined up in this formation, and saw the Sam follow the flat route, so the Oregon staff felt they could create a running lane in the alley inside of where the Sam ended up after following the flat route.

Oregon Drive 7 / Play 2 / 2ⁿᵈ & 8 / -28 Yard Line / Right Hash / 4:38 2Q

Oregon 7 – OSU 21

Summary

Holding Penalty for 10 yards

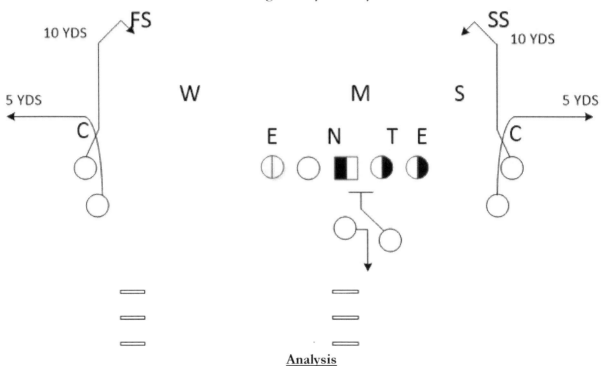

Analysis

The offense is looking to attack the flats because of Ohio State's refusal to switch on routes like these. The safety will still come over the top.

Point man tries to rub the outside linebacker to get the flat route open to the boundary, but press coverage from the corner pushed him too far inside.

The stacked alignment acts as a disadvantage for the #2 receiver to the boundary and the Sam linebacker as deep enough to come over the top of #1 vertical route. At this point, it probably makes more sense for the #1 receiver to get vertical right away to better wall of the outside linebacker instead of taking an inside release.

Mariota reads boundary flat to short curl.

Oregon Drive 7 / Play 3 / 2nd & 18 / -18 Yard Line / Right Hash / 4:20 2Q
Oregon 7 – OSU 21
Summary

Pass complete to Marshall for a 7 yard gain

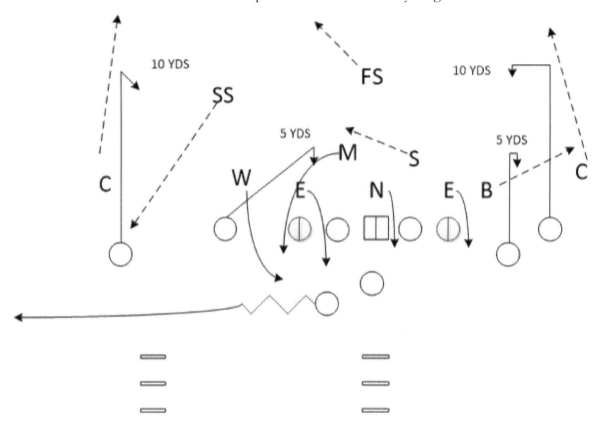

Analysis

Once he recognizes the pressure, Mariota is trying to get the ball to the Y as quickly as possible as he runs a route to replace the blitzing linebacker, but the route takes too long to develop and Mariota works to the opposite side of the formation to the slot receiver.

As the offense sends the back in wide motion before the snap, only the strong safety widens since the two linebackers to the field side are assigned to come on a field pressure.

Oregon Drive 7 / Play 4 / 3rd & 11 / -24 Yard Line / Right Hash / 4:06 2Q
Oregon 7 – OSU 21
Summary

Pass complete to Stanford for a gain of 28 yards and a first down

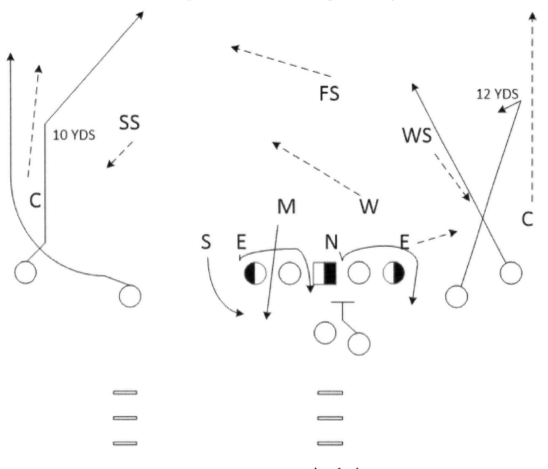

Analysis

The ball is thrown just as the receiver clears the boundary safety. Mariota is hoping to get the ball to his receivers in a tight window in between the free and weak safety. He is throwing opposite of the drop of the middle linebacker, who in this case is the Will dropping into the short middle.

I don't like the read by Mariota, the free safety is playing the short side of the field too tight for the route, can get the receiver killed. There's an inside vertical running free down the seam wide open but Mariota doesn't even look to that side of the field.

Oregon Dive 7 / Play 5 / 1st & 10 / +48 Yard Line / Right Hash / 3:50 2Q
Oregon 7 – OSU 21

Summary
Thomas Tyner runs for a gain of 3 yards.

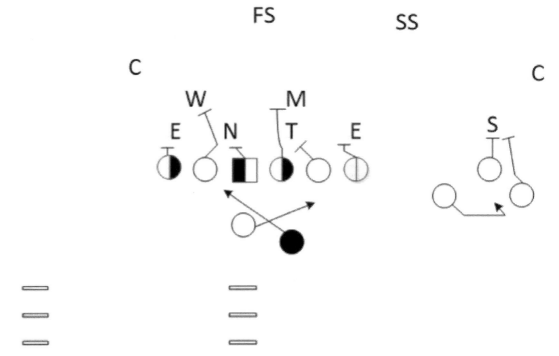

Analysis

This is the same idea as the offensive line identifying the blitz key when lining up the tight end on the opposite side of the 3x1 formation on previous drives, only this time the three receiver side is lined up into the short side of the field.

The defensive end lined up over the tight end still causes problems by slanting to the inside gap, and the offense is looking to set up a cutback run to the short side of the field. Their goal is opening up the alley off the tight end by removing the Sam linebacker from the equation. The offense is hoping that he'll remove himself by aligning over the bunch formation, and that's exactly what happens.

Oregon Drive 7 / Play 6 / 2ⁿᵈ & 7 / +45 Yard Line / Right Hash / 3:37 2Q
Oregon 7 – OSU 21

Summary
Pass complete to Byron Marshall for a gain of 15 yards

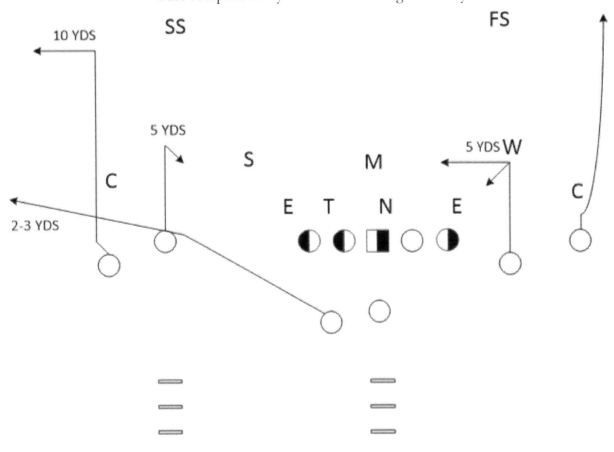

Analysis

The #2 receiver to the field side is there to rub the on the outside linebacker flying out to the flat. The Mike linebacker flies out to the 3 receiver side to get the 4 on 3 advantage, and the option route by the slot receiver attacks the middle of the field which is suddenly wide open.

The left side of the formation is the first read, since Mariota wants to see how the defense will cover the flat route out of the backfield and whether they'll move anyone, especially the Mike linebacker. Once again he reads the Mike and throws to the opposite side of the field, where the slot receiver has timed up his option route to come open over the middle of the field and attack where the Mike used to be.

Oregon Drive 7 / Play 7/ 1st & 10 / +30 Yard Line / Right Hash / 3:18 2Q
Oregon 7 – OSU 21
Summary
Sack! Mariota sacked for a loss of 1 yard.

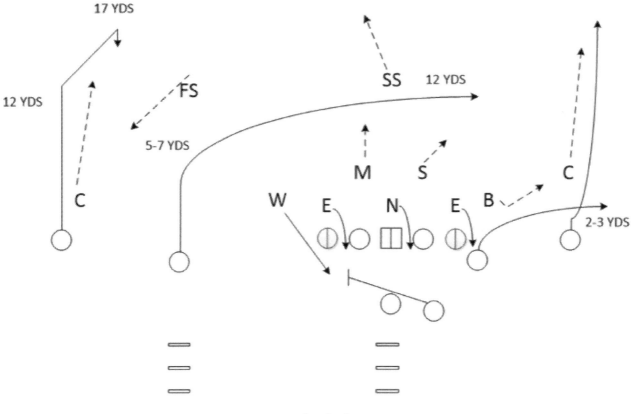

Analysis

The Z receiver is running a true fade route where he lines up at the top of the numbers, and ends up about two yards outside the numbers looking for the hole shot from the QB. The defense brings some edge pressure from the wide side of the field, and the stand up defensive end to the boundary is dropping to the flat on that side.

When Mariota is flushed away from the pocket, he scrambles to the field and only one receiver to side is open, the X receiver running the curl, but Mariota can't set his feet get in the right position to throw. He's forced out of bounds instead.

Oregon Drive 7 / Play 8 / 2ⁿᵈ & 11 / +31 Yard Line / Left Hash / 3:00 2Q
Oregon 7 – OSU 21
Summary
Mariota runs for a 2 yard gain

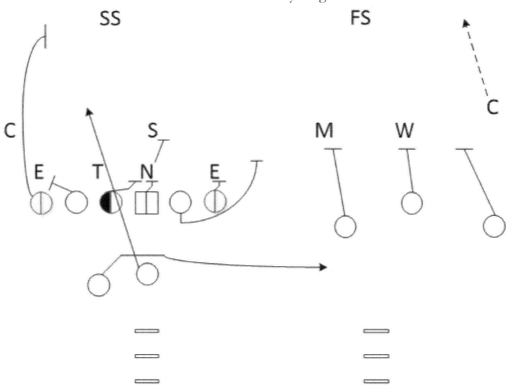

Analysis

This is Oregon's version of the classic midline play that is a staple of option offenses, which reads the defensive tackle and forces him to play more disciplined and hesitate. The offensive line does not account for the corner in the blocking scheme, even when he's right near the line of scrimmage.

The three technique defensive tackle comes up the field and technically turns his shoulders to close down on the tailback, but he's got the speed to reverse course and forces Mariota to get to the sideline instead of getting through the hole. Ideally, the quarterback should 'replace the read' on this play, meaning end up where the defender was lined up pre-snap. This is a common way to coach up the midline play for many coaches who run it on a regular basis.

It's interesting to note that the defense doesn't really change up their alignment, just widens their linebackers against spread formations for it.

Oregon Drive 7 / Play 9 / 2nd & 9 / -29 Yard Line / Left Hash / 2:29 2Q
Oregon 7 – OSU 21
Summary
Pass complete to Charles Nelson for a gain of 14 yards and a first down

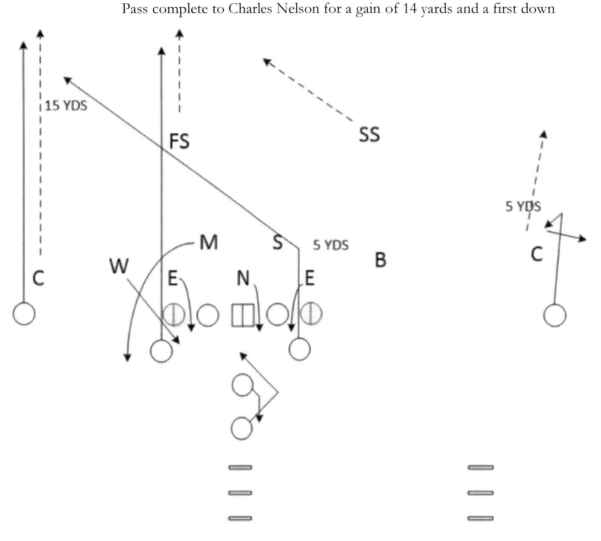

Analysis

The corner to the boundary uses a shuffle technique and once he gets past the 15 yard mark, he's expecting someone else to come into that space. He's in the area to collapse on the crossing route. Two routes to the boundary just going vertical and opening up a large hole to the boundary side at about 12-15 yards.

Once again we see Ohio State bring pressure on 3rd and long, opening up space for a completion at an intermediate depth. The receiver gets drilled, but manages to hang on to the ball.

This pressure from the boundary against this full-house look is a great complement to the corner blitz what Ohio State has been running.

<u>Oregon Drive 7 / Play 10 / 1st & 10 / -15 Yard Line / Left Hash / 1:59 2Q</u>
Oregon 7 – OSU 21
<u>Summary</u>
Royce Freeman runs for a gain of 3 yards

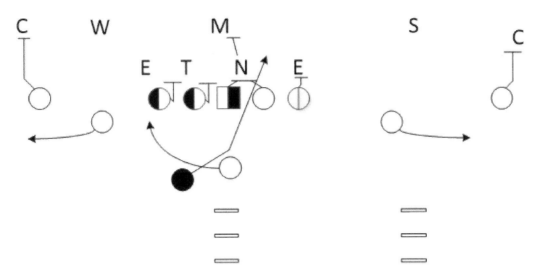

<u>Analysis</u>

Here comes the inside zone play again, with Oregon trying to move the ball on the ground using one-back formations.

Head up 4 tech to the field is bouncing the plays outside to the linebackers, gets his head in the inside gap. This also frees up the inside linebacker to come after the ball.

It's a bad read by the tailback, if he stays patient on the left side he'll see a large running lane develop on as the defensive tackle comes across the face of the guard and leaves his gap open.

The defense is very good at giving looks that trick the back into thinking there is a lot of room on the edge, only for it to disappear very quickly.

Oregon Drive 7 / Play 11 / 2nd & 7 / +12 Yard Line / Middle / 1:40 2Q
Oregon 7 – OSU 21
Summary
Royce Freeman runs for a gain of 3 yards.

SS   10-12 YDS   FS

C   S   M   C

E   T   N   E   W

Analysis

The blocking scheme of the zone read allows the back to hit up inside even if the defense aligns away from the back. In this case, the zero technique on the center means that the right guard and right tackle can combo out to the edge LB and forms a wall that seals off the outside defender, and creates a running lane up the middle. It puts a body on the outside linebacker in the alley and may make it a bit easier for the back to hit the hole wider.

Vertical route by #2 holds backside safety. In case the defensive end forces the QB to pull the ball, the progression is flat to drag to run. The safety to the TE side comes down to play the QB, and would've vacated the space where the receiver ended up wide open in the end zone.

Oregon Drive 7 / Play 12 / 3rd & 4 / +9 Yard Line / Middle / 1:12 2Q
Oregon 7 – OSU 21
Summary
Incomplete pass

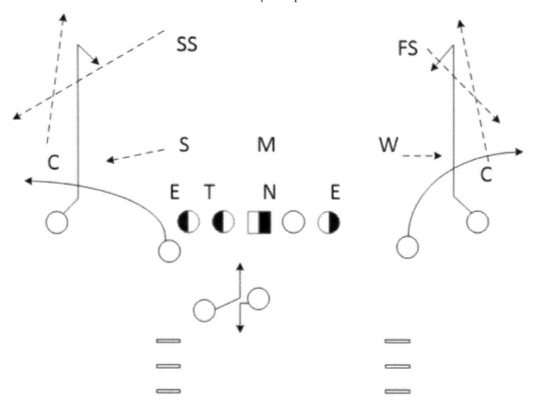

Analysis

Because of the coverage and Ohio State's refusal to adjust to this formation, Oregon goes back to something that they've had a lot of success with in this game.

The defensive end chips the TE as he's releasing off the line of scrimmage, and it has a lot to do with why the pass is incomplete. Still, the TE is very much wide open.

In the middle of the field, when there is no short side of the field, and when the Mike linebacker doesn't declare a side after the snap, Mariota's default side is the side of the formation where the back is lined up, since he has to open up the that side first to complete the playfake.

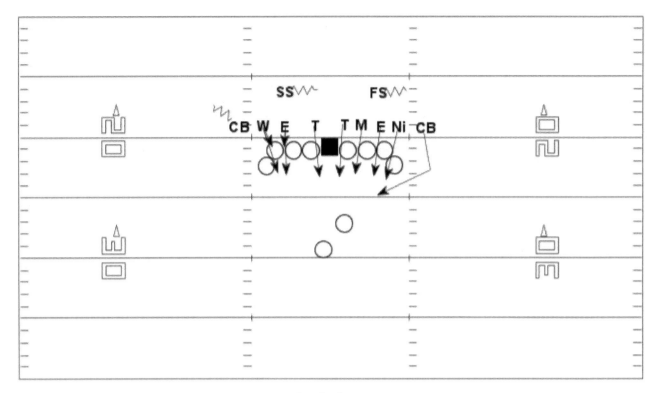

Analysis

The right wing for Oregon doesn't even touch the edge rusher coming wide off the right side. The corner's job is to come right off the butt of the rusher.

Oregon Drive #7 Review

<u>Oregon</u>

It still seems like Oregon is grasping for straws in the run game this half, having never settled on a consistent scheme or formation. They have had some success in the intermediate passing game down the seams, especially on 3rd down. It seems like Oregon is determined to make the inside zone work somehow and keep throwing out different versions of it, yet the opposite is true in the pass game.

<u>Ohio State</u>

The Buckeyes played a style of bend-but-don't-break defense, and didn't give up many yards except for on third down, when they brought pressure, which backfired and opened up space down the field.

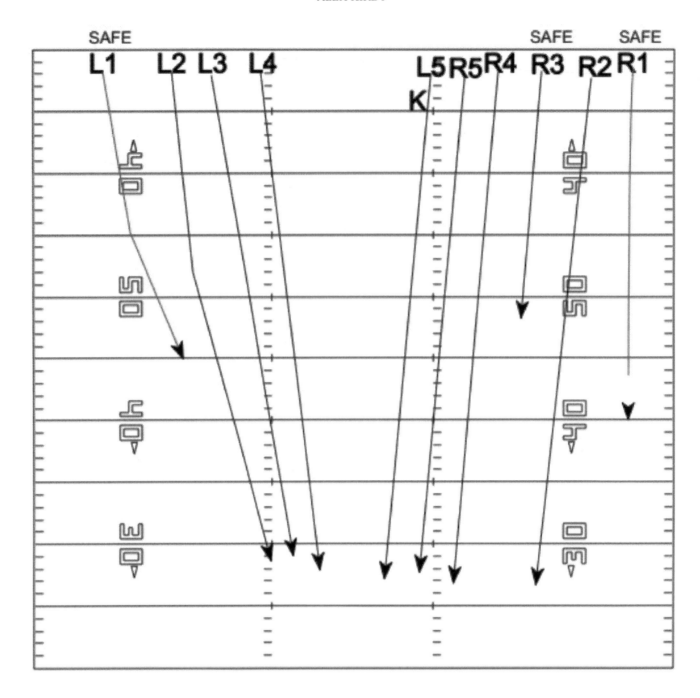

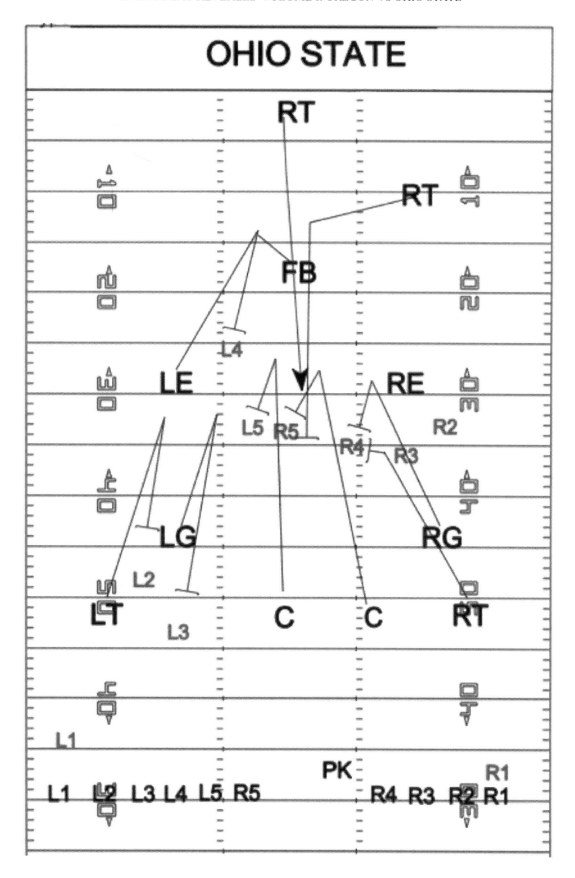

Ohio State Drive 7 / Play 1 / 1st & 10 / -13 Yard Line / Left Hash / 0:48 2Q
Oregon 7 – OSU 21
Summary
Elliott runs for a gain of 1 yard

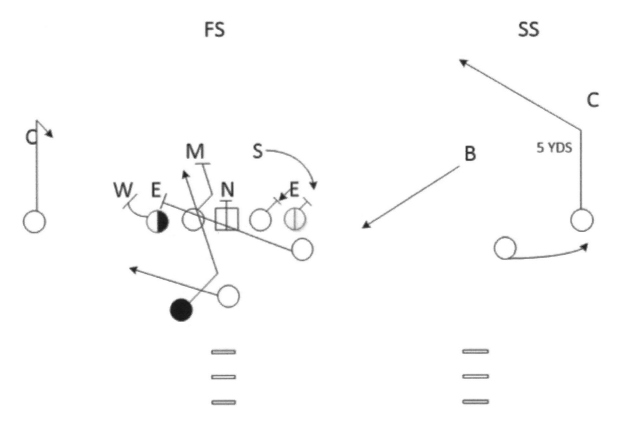

Analysis

The weak side defensive end in the 4i technique does a great job coming off the butt of the left guard, once he sees his outside leg move to block down on the center on the combo. He closes the amount of open space inside on the wham play, and the left guard is out-maneuvered at the next level by the Mike linebacker and the back tries to cut it back, which means that he's stuffed at the line because the playside inside linebacker isn't blocked.

The nose forces the back to cutback because he beats the center across his face (the left guard is lazy on the combo block).

Another interesting principle is the importance of the running back "pressing" the line of scrimmage, meaning that he gets closer, bringing the linebackers up closer to the line and making it easier for the blockers up front.

Ohio State Drive 7 / Play 2 / 2nd & 10 / -13 Yard Line / Left Hash / 0:31 2Q
Oregon 10 – OSU 21
Summary
Elliott runs for a gain of 3 yards

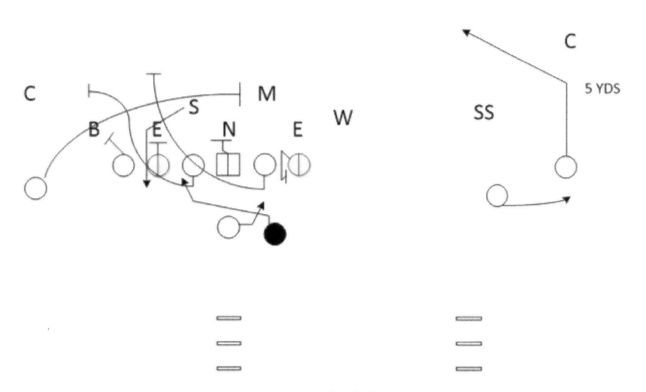

Analysis

It seems like Oregon is making a habit of blitzing the strong side of the Ace formation because of the tendencies for the pin and pull.

On this play the Sam dominates the C gap and cuts off the pulling guard and forces a cutback to the Will linebacker.

This is a problem that Ohio State needs to solve, because even with their success on the ground, they're becoming more and more predictable, and the defensive front is able to play faster and without hesitation.

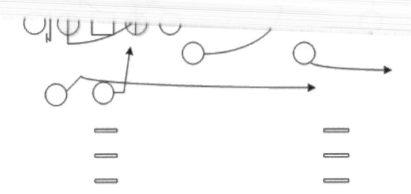

Analysis

The adjustment by the front seven to bump over the defensive line pays dividends on this play. The defensive end over the pulling guard comes over the top of the center's block and helps stop the QB run before it has a chance to really get going.

The right tackle does a great job of coming off of the combo and sealing off the Mike linebacker who over runs the play by chasing the guard.

The unbalanced formation putting four receivers is designed to stretch the interior defenders and open up a crease inside.

RUGBY PUNT

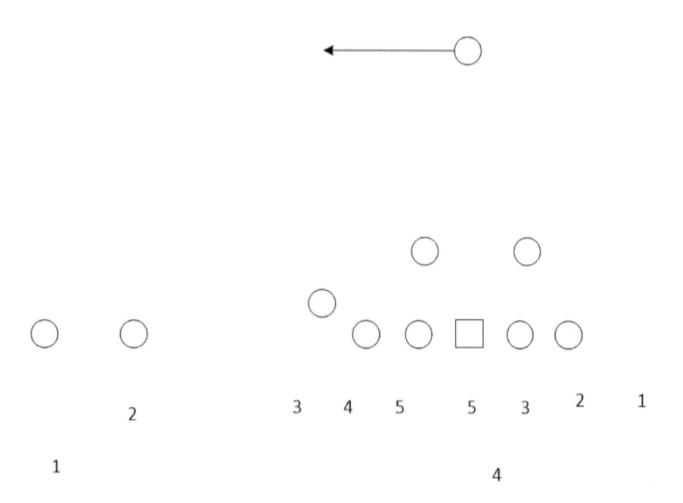

<u>Analysis</u>

The rugby punt is designed for the ball to come off the punter's foot awkwardly , which makes it tough to catch, and can make it roll in the kicking team's favor.

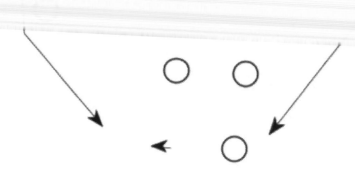

Analysis

Oregon is playing a safe return scheme and forcing the returner is coached up to fair catch the ball no matter what to conserve time.

Ohio State Drive #7 Review

<u>Ohio State</u>

This was a case of Ohio State going back to what worked best so far in this game and Oregon being ready for it. They're just trying to pick up the 1st down and get out of the half alive. What they did not want is to have to punt the ball back to Oregon with prime field position, and that's exactly what happens.

<u>Oregon</u>

Despite the early troubles, right now Oregon has this run game figured out. The defensive line is playing extremely well, and the guys up front are playing fast. Fortunately for the Ducks, Ohio State didn't try to challenge them down the field.

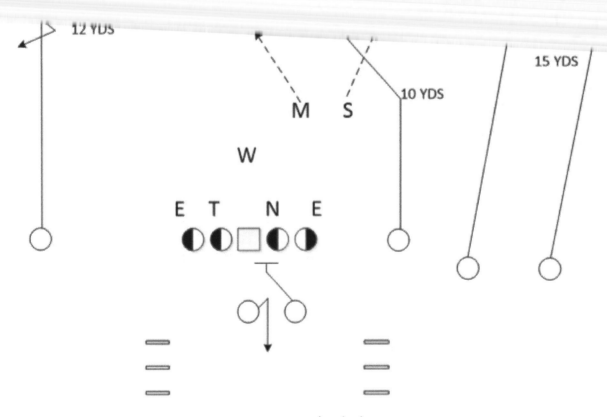

12 YDS

15 YDS

10 YDS

M   S

W

E   T   N   E

Analysis

It's an interesting alignment by the two LBs to the trips side, as they're at 4 yards deeper than the other linebacker, I presume to take care of any vertical crossing routes.

The offense is targeting the sidelines, relying on the seam routes to occupy the middle of the field, and create one-on-one matchups with a large cushion.

<u>Oregon Drive 8 / Play 2 / 1st & 10 / -45 Yard Line / Left Hash / 0:09 2Q</u>
Oregon 10 – OSU 21
<u>Summary</u>
Pass complete to Tyner for a gain of 3 yards, lateraled to Marshall for a gain of 1 yard

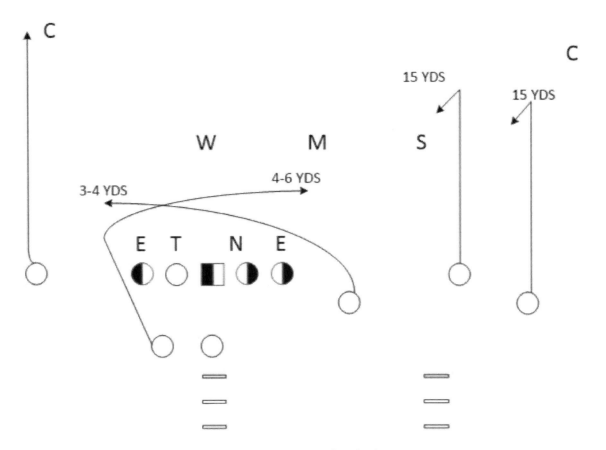

<u>Analysis</u>
This is a pretty low-risk, high-reward play here. The offense is basically hoping for a miracle, and they've given themselves two opportunities for a big play after a lateral, one on each side of the formation. Mariota can throw the curls to the wide side of the field in order to let them lateral to the shallow crossing receiver coming from the opposite side of the field, or more immediately he can throw to the back angling out of the backfield and let him pitch the ball to the slot receiver coming across from the right side.

Oregon Halftime Review

Problems They Have

the middle linebacker.
- They've been able to create rubs on defenders, especially out of stacked receiver alignments, and get receivers open in the flat.

Ohio State Halftime Review

Problems They Have

- They want to be able to run off-tackle in the C gap, but their best plays have become too predictable out of the same formations. They need to create some hesitation and misdirection at the point of attack.
- They need to create some additional answers in the passing game, since as complex and varied as they've been with the number of run schemes, the pass game has been largely limited to crossing routes, boots, and run-adjust passes.
- Cardale hasn't done well when he's had to stand back, drop and throw. Oregon has gotten pressure on him, forced him out of the pocket, taken him out of his progression.

What They've Done Well

- Cardale has done best with simple reads, reads where he can keep his eyes in one area of the field and not have to reset his body as he goes through the progression.
- They have created some open seams using gap schemes by pulling the linemen and tight end off the line of scrimmage.
- The throws to the wide side of the field on hitch screens and run adjust passes have forced the defense to account for them, which in turn opens up space in the run game.

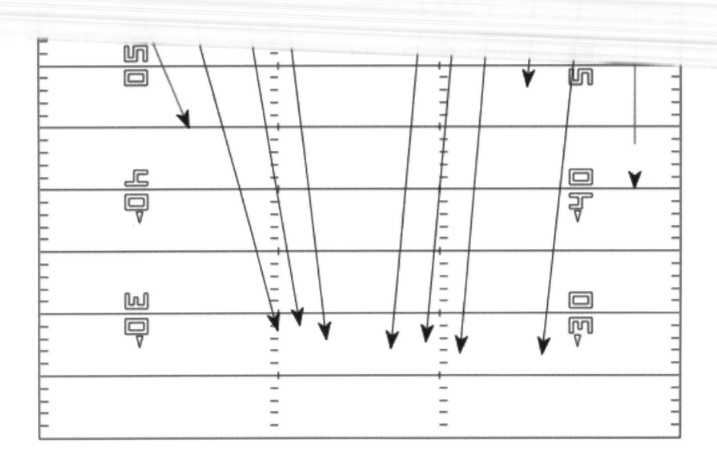

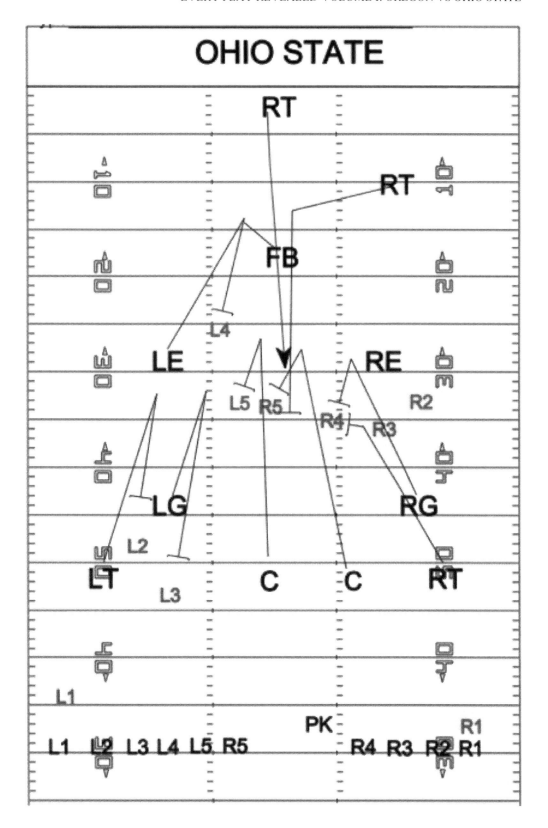

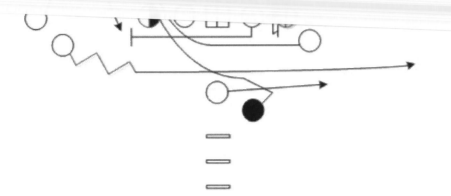

Analysis

The offense uses the stacked receiver alignment to the boundary in order to put the Will linebacker in conflict and widen him out to open up running lanes for the counter play up inside.

The jet motion by the slot receiver coming across the formation forces the safeties to adjust and holds the backside inside linebacker just long enough for the offensive line to seal him off from the gap up the middle.

The Mike linebacker is frozen in place by the motion, which allows the pullers to create a running lane to the open side. This is the first instance of the counter play in this game, right out of halftime, and it solves the problem we talked about by creating defensive hesitation and keeping the defense honest at the point of attack.

Ohio State Drive 8 / Play 2 / 1st & 10 / -47 Yard Line / Left Hash / 14:53 3Q
Oregon 10 – OSU 21

Summary
Cardale Jones runs for a gain of 5 yards.

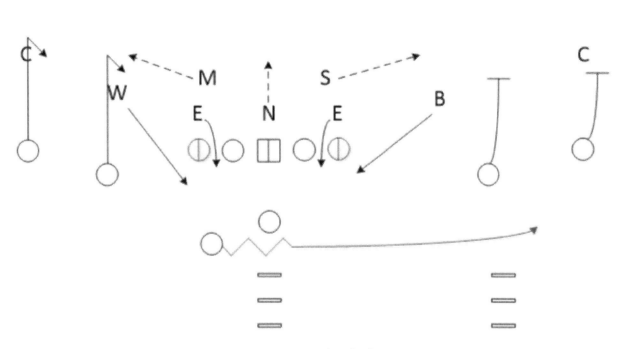

Analysis

The offense wants to get the ball out in space, so they come back to the flare screen once again.

Cardale sees the Will coming and looks off the coverage to the flare side before coming back and trying to throw the double hitch side.

Oregon comes with more edge pressure from the outside linebacker position, while the two inside linebackers widen out to undercut any kind of shallow throw like the hitch routes that are developing to the boundary.

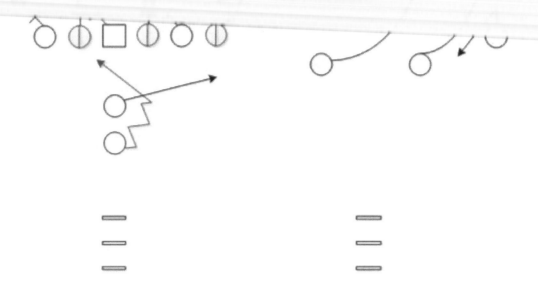

Analysis

The aiming point is the left guard, and the defensive end aligned over the tight end comes around and makes the tackle from behind once he clears the tight end's arc block. Still, the back hits the strong side A gap and picks up the first down.

This is an example of a halftime adjustment that the Buckeyes have put into practice. The defensive end over the tight end has been causing them a lot of trouble out of this formation, since with his quickness off the snap he's been able to penetrate and disrupt the run game, even when they run away from him. As a result, the offense has decided to release the tight end on an "arc" block away from the direction of the play in the hope of slowing down and widening out the defensive end and nullify the backside pursuit. It works well enough for the offense to pick up the first down.

Ohio State Drive 8 / Play 5 / 1st & 10 / +42 Yard Line / Left Hash / 13:55 3Q
Oregon 10 – OSU 21
Summary
Incomplete pass

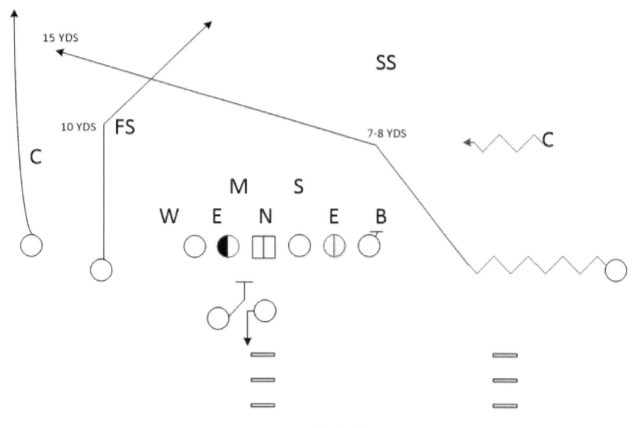

Analysis

The Z receiver is knocked off his route by the outside linebacker (B) and is removed from the play since he can't come across the formation in time to have any effect on the two vertical routes to the opposite side of the field.

His eyes are locked in to the left side of the field and when he sees the X receiver in single coverage to the boundary and nearly throws the TD pass play but it's out of bounds by only a few inches.

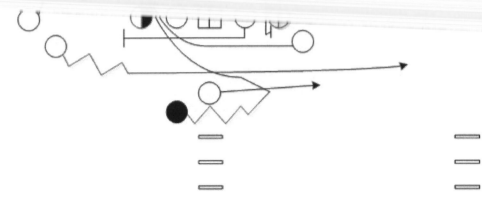

Analysis

This is one of the rare times when the offense sends two different players in motion at two separate times. First the tailback flips from one side of the quarterback to the other in the backfield, then once he has been set for at least one second, Cardale will send the second motion man on a jet sweep path into the backfield. It ends up becoming the exact same play and alignment as the first counter play on this drive.

The Mike linebacker comes downhill and the Y comes tight off the butt of left tackle and kicks out the Mike creating a running lane inside. The strong safety ends up making the tackle even after being momentarily frozen by the receiver coming across to that side of the formation with the jet sweep motion.

Ohio State Drive 8 / Play 6 / 3rd & 2 / +34 Yard Line / Left Hash / 13:07 3Q
Oregon 10 – OSU 21
Summary
Elliott runs for a gain of 1 yard

FS   SS

C

C

M   S

W   E   N   E   B

Analysis

The unblocked defensive end slants to the side of the play and the right tackle doesn't come off the combination to the Will linebacker, the linebacker then shuts down the zone read and the ball carrier's path forcing 4th down.

Another thing to note is that Oregon has adjusted their defensive alignment against this unbalanced look from Ohio State. Where before the three down linemen had lined up over the tight end and two guards, on this play they return to their traditional alignments, with the nose over the center and the defensive ends over each offensive tackle.

Analysis

This at first looks to be a regular old fashioned quarterback sneak, but when his first attempt to pick up the first down fails, Cardale pulls up and manages to beat the Will linebacker to the edge to pick up the first down, but not before taking a good hit from the corner as he hurdles for the first down.

The offensive line is foot-to-foot with their splits, and at the snap they'll each take their first step to protect their inside gap. The defense is also packed in pretty tight as well, with the outside linebackers shaded on the outside shoulder of the tight end on either side of the formation to protect against just the kind of play that Cardale pulls off here.

Ohio State Drive 8 / Play 8 / 1st & 15 / +37 Yard Line / Left Hash / 11:52 3Q
Oregon 10 – OSU 21
Summary
Pass intercepted by Oregon

FS

15-17 YDS

C

SS

5 YDS

B

C

M   S

W   E   N   E

Analysis

(This play immediately follows a false start penalty)

The ball is thrown behind the receiver on the out route, and he has to adjust awkwardly and can't hold on to the ball, it bounces around and it's intercepted by the defender. It's designed to get the quarterback on the edge, but the rusher coming from the outside to step up and deliver the football before he's ready. Both the quarterback and the receiver share blame on this play.

that Ohio State has been running to the

Oregon did a great job of forcing another turnover and giving the ball back to the offense.

Oregon Drive 9 / Play 1 / 1ˢᵗ & 10 / -30 Yard Line / Left Hash / 11:33 3Q
Oregon 10 – OSU 21
Summary

Touchdown! Mariota completes to Marshall for a gain of 70 yards and a score.

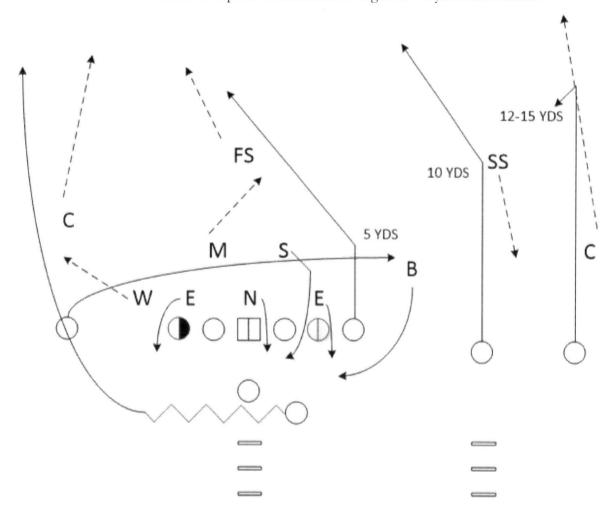

Analysis

Oregon goes right back to what has worked best right out of the gate. The Ducks go right after the defense in the middle of the field. The tight end post occupies the free safety to the opposite side, and with the strong safety rotating down low in Cover 3, there's a big gap along the deep right hash.

We see this problem again and again in this game, no one disrupts the receiver going down the middle. Ohio State hasn't done a good job all game of disrupting vertical routes and they don't do it here either.

Ohio State comes with field pressure while the defensive end dropping to the flat in the boundary does a marvelous job of touching no one. The boundary corner drops and opens up facing away from the sideline.

POLE CAT FORMATION

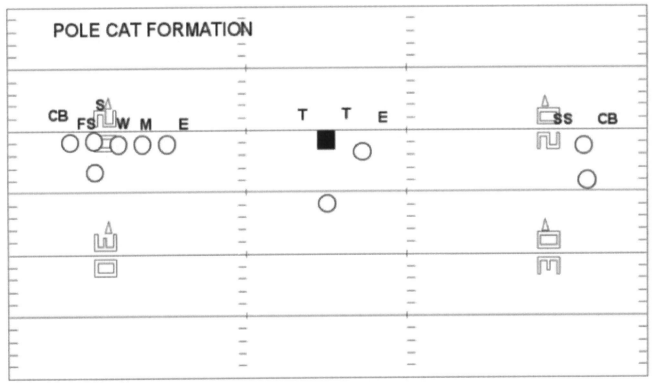

Oregon Drive #9 Review

Oregon

The Z receiver runs the deep curl route instead of running a vertical route to the wide side of the field that will never be a legitimate threat to catch the ball. Why take yourself out of the play? Beyond a certain point, you're running yourself out of the quarterback's range. I like the way this route concept is designed.

Ohio State

Ohio State comes with field pressure and the SS isn't in a good spot to disrupt the #2 receiver seam route, and he goes right down the middle.

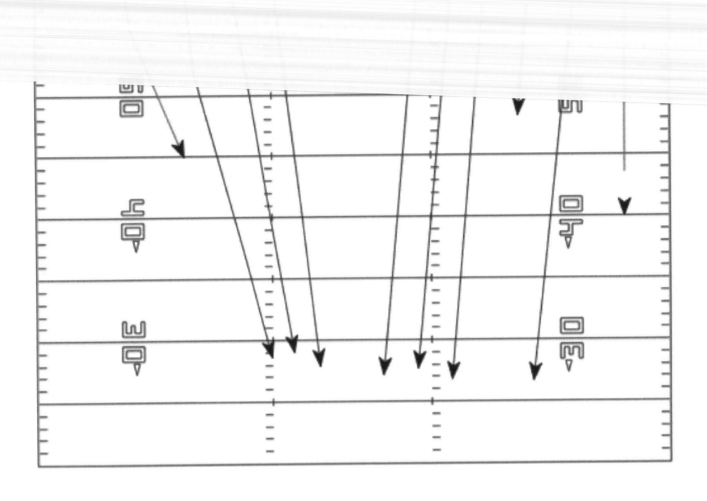

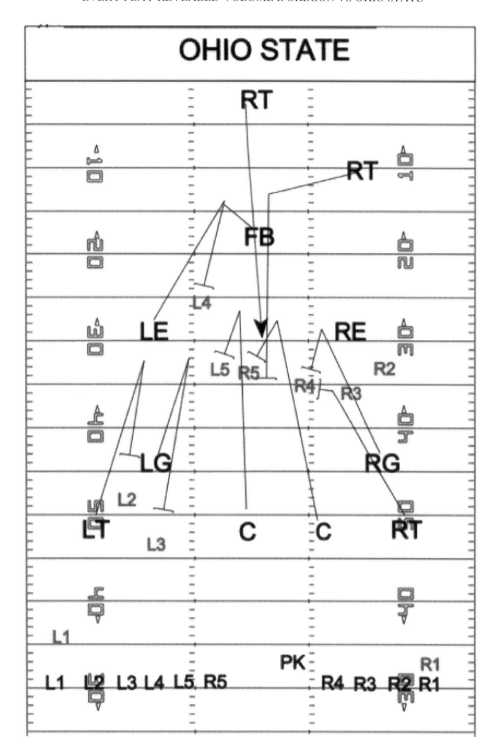

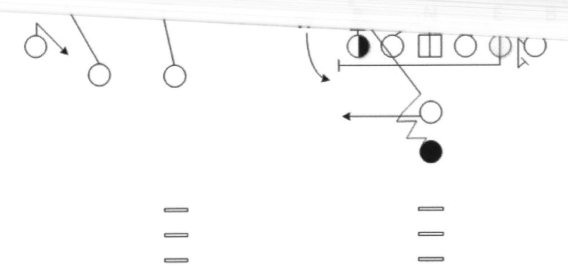

Analysis

Ohio State goes right back to what's been working for much of the game, and it goes for a 15 yard gain and a 1st down.

The tailback starts off in the pistol then shifts into the offset position on the left, and the Will blitzer slips and falls when coming off the edge so that the puller doesn't have anyone to kick out. This play is a good response to the edge blitzes that Oregon is bringing against this formation.

Ohio State Drive 9 / Play 2 / 1st & 10 / -38 Yard Line / Right Hash / 11:16 3Q
Oregon 17 – OSU 21

Summary
Cardale Jones is stopped in the backfield for a loss of 1 yard

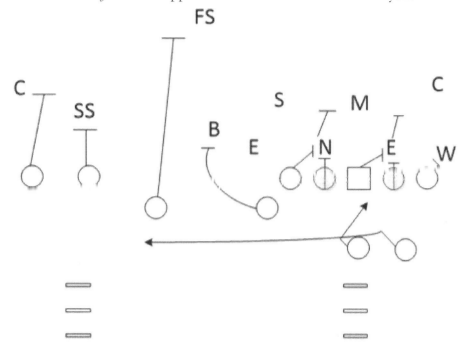

Analysis

Cardale is going to the opposite combo block on the right side of the offensive line and would've had a decent gain had the corner not been able to shoot through the offensive line. The right guard doesn't account for the corner shooting through the B gap, and he ends up making the tackle.

This is the first time Ohio State has run their inverted zone read scheme, where the QB and the tailback exchange responsibilities, since when the defensive end closes down the line the quarterback will give the ball and let the back get out on the edge.

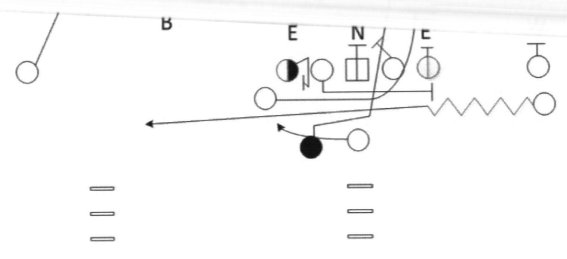

Analysis

Once again, the stacked receiver set opens everything up off-tackle for the offense.

The right guard and center do a great job of turning the nose tackle, opening up the B gap, the Mike linebacker gets outside of the guard, opening up space inside.

The jet motion, combined with the quarterback mesh with the running back takes the Sam to scrape to the backfield.

Ohio State Drive 9 / Play 4 / 3ʳᵈ & 3 / -45 Yard Line / Right Hash / 10:14 3Q
Oregon 17 – OSU 21
Summary
Cardale Jones runs for a gain of 2 yards

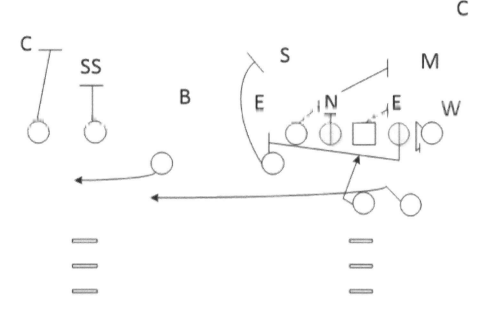

Analysis

Cardale is very eager to cut to the backside A-gap similar to the way a running back would do against this look.

The bubble route serves to widen the strong outside linebacker to that side, and effectively "block" him by removing him from the equation. At the same time, the pulling guard kicks out the defensive end and the H-back seals off the Sam linebacker from the interior of the play.

There isn't much movement on the backside of the play, but they get it close enough so that the offense can make a reasonable attempt at converting a 4th and 1 on the next play.

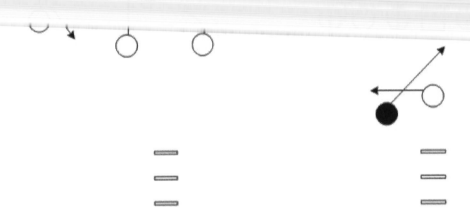

Analysis

The strong side defensive end crosses the face of the tight end and even though the tailback makes the right read, he's tackled by that defensive end because of the lack of space in the backfield.

Still, it's enough to pick up the 1st down by just a hair.

Oregon Drive 9 / Play 6 / 1st & 10 / -49 Yard Line / Right Hash / 8:53 3Q
Oregon 17 – OSU 21

Summary
Cardale is sacked and fumbles the ball, recovered by Oregon

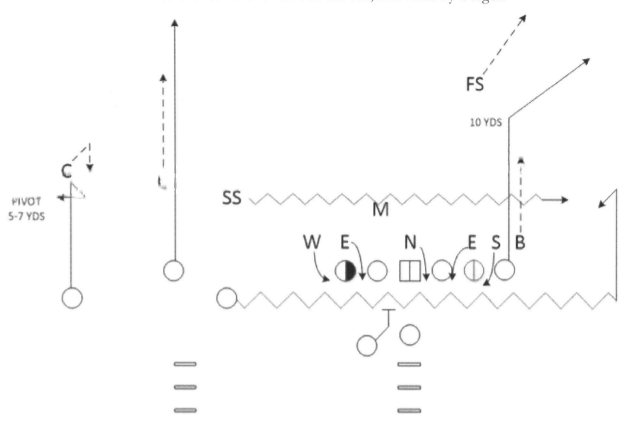

Analysis

Cardale is eyeing the smash side the entire way. The tight end is mugged coming off the line of scrimmage and Cardale is waiting for the corner route to come open, but is flushed from the pocket and loses the football when trying to get rid of it and throwing it away.

A lot of this has to do with what we talked about earlier, the defense is interested in taking away the short side of the field. The free safety and strong outside linebacker are doubling the corner route by the tight end, and the strong safety is blanketing the hitch route on the outside. The pressure flushes Cardale out of the pocket while his eyes are locked in on the tight end waiting for the corner route to come open, and he ends up losing his balance, as well as the football, and giving Oregon a much needed takeaway that keeps them in the game.

- The Ducks run

- They've already been given a chance to end the drive on 4th down, but could go up front.

- The one pass Ohio State throws on the drive ends up in disaster, because Oregon's defense brackets the short side of the field.

Oregon Drive 10 / Play 1 / 1ˢᵗ & 10 / +23 Yard Line / Left Hash / 8:21 3Q
Oregon 17 – OSU 21
Summary

Marshall runs for a gain of 9 yards

FS   SS

C

W   M   S

C

F   N   E

Analysis

Oregon motions to an unbalanced Y-off two-back to force the defense to widen and open up space in the alley.

The tight end takes a poor angle for the inside linebacker. Instead of aiming for where he is, he should release wide enough to cut off the pursuit of the defender. If he gets a better angle, this play can be cut up the middle and this is a much bigger play. Still, it's a great pickup on 1st down.

They're playing formation games with the Sam linebacker, so if he splits the difference between #2 and the offensive tackle, they can always throw the hitch screen to the wide side of the field or pull the front side guard on a stretch play.

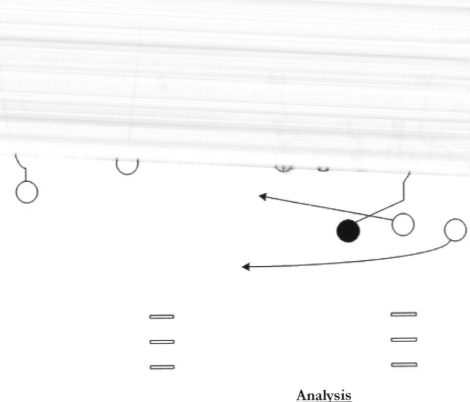

Analysis

This is the first time the offense is unbalanced twin in a two-back gun.

The corner is very physical to the open side. It makes the whole defensive scheme work when you as a defense can spill a play outside to a corner who isn't afraid to stick his nose in the pile.

The four technique to the boundary forces the ball outside to the LB and CB. This is a great call on in a short-yardage situation, relies on the over pursuit, or sucking in of the defenders.

In my opinion, this isn't the best use of a two-back formation. If you're going to line up in this unbalanced look out of two backs, why run the same inside zone scheme that has the same issues that your normal zone scheme has been facing all game, specifically forcing the ball to bounce outside to an edge defender, and the corner plays very physical.

Oregon Drive 10 / Play 3 / 1ˢᵗ & 10 / +12 Yard Line / Right Hash / 7:56 3Q
Oregon 17 – OSU 21
Summary
Tyner is stopped in the backfield for a loss of 2 yards

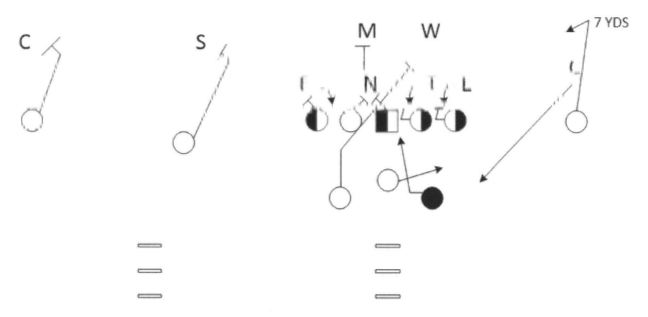

Analysis

Oregon is trying to run the same two-back isolation play from the first quarter, but the corner blitz means that the defensive line to that side starts inside. You can tell that the right guard and right tackle are blocking out in a man scheme and aren't in a good position to deal with the defensive line slanting across their faces. This shuts down the play from the get go.

Ohio State comes with the corner blitz from the boundary. Interesting that the defensive end away from the corner blitz slants inside for the purpose of bouncing the play outside to the linebacker, which is not what you normally see on the opposite side of an edge blitz.

This has been one of Ohio State's consistent answers to the two-back run game from Oregon.

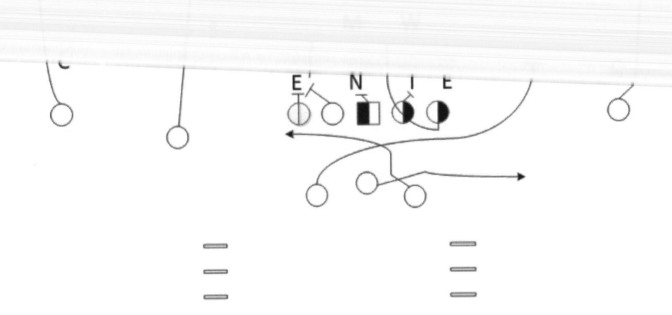

Analysis

The X receiver does a very clever thing to take the corner with him on this play. Basically simulates a route from a run-pass option. The tackle's pull holds the play side inside linebacker a second longer, just long enough for the arcing back out of the backfield can get in good position to have a change on the edge.

The defense is playing a Cover 4 when the safety has the responsibility to come downhill instead of the corner, which is great for the offense. They've used the formation to clear the alley to the boundary and open up running room to the short side of the field.

It's an interesting scheme from the offensive line on this play, as the fold inside by the tackle create an added element of misdirection, and gives the Will linebacker a false key.

Oregon Drive 10 / Play 5 / 3rd & 3 / +5 Yard Line / Right Hash / 7:09 3Q
Oregon 17 – OSU 21
Summary
Incomplete pass

Analysis

Ohio State comes with a corner blitz right into the face of Mariota so that he neither has the time to wait for the back of the end zone to come open, nor the angle to scramble around. It doesn't do much good to run the other way because all of the receivers are on the boundary side of the field.

The routes on the back side, either because of design or by mistake, are not properly spaced out. If the Z gets shallow and more horizontal he can probably reach the window past the right hash that would've been a very easy throw for a touchdown.

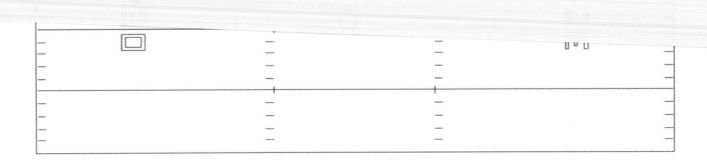

Oregon Drive #10 Review

Oregon

• Oregon clearly made a conscious effort to get back into two-back sets and force the defense to account for a lead back, and get the ball inside, though the call on 3rd and 3 is puzzling, simply because it seems like a call a coach makes when he's going to go for it on 4th down.

• The offensive staff for Oregon clearly decided that this was an appropriate time to experiment with two backs, because even if it doesn't work out, the offense is still in field goal range

Ohio State

• Ohio State came with the answer once Oregon tried to attack the short side of the field. It has less to do with the standing inside of the offensive line to force this play outside

• The They layout have accomplished exactly what they set out to do, by forcing Oregon to get away from their primary game plan.

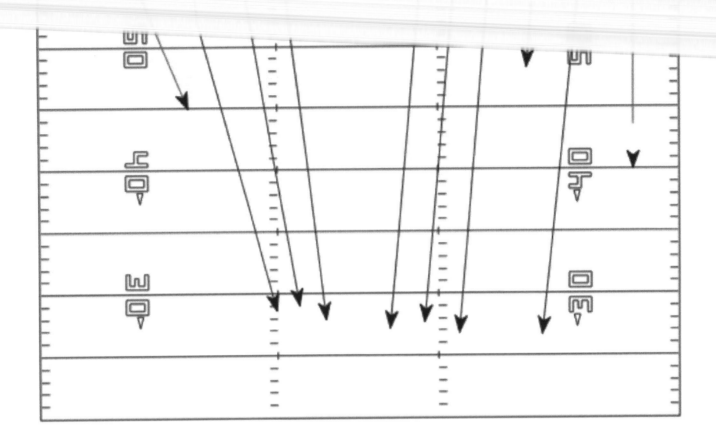

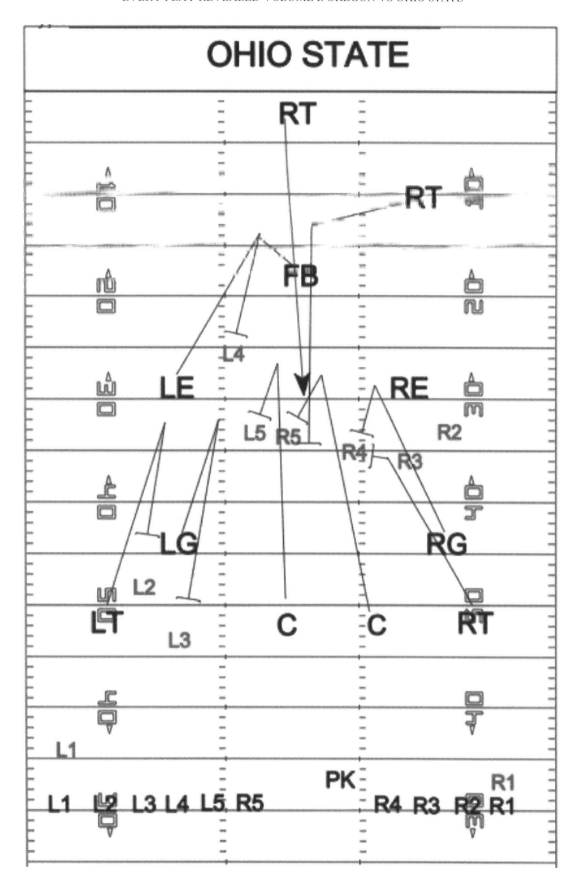

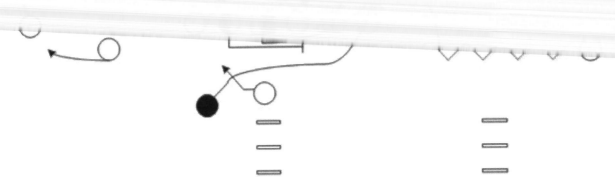

Analysis

Once again, the Buckeyes start the drive with a gap scheme like this one, the pin and pull.

Cardale changes the play at the line of scrimmage because of instructions from the sideline. The center pulls instead of the right guard which allows the right guard to get a good angle on the one technique defensive tackle. It's basically an under front with the Will linebacker acting as the five technique defensive end on the open side.

Sam linebacker shoots through the open gap to his side and takes out the left guard, which forces the play wider than its original design.

The Z receiver doesn't have anyone to block because the Sam shot through the gap, and he ends up chasing the back down from behind and making the tackle.

Ohio State Drive 10 / Play 2 / 2nd & 2 / -33 Yard Line / Right Hash / 6:23 3Q
Oregon 20 – OSU 21
Summary
Elliott runs for a gain of 4 yards and a first down

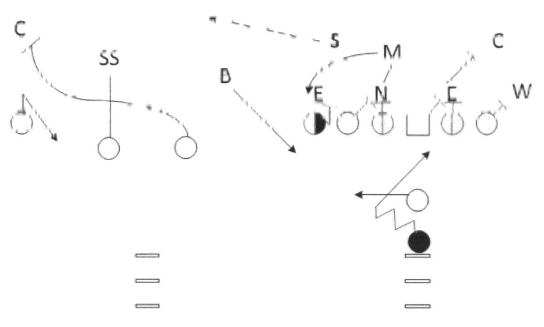

Analysis

Once again the defensive end comes across the tight end's face to disrupt the inside zone play. He slants inside aggressively because of the edge rusher coming from the slot. The Mike linebacker also comes from the field as part of the field pressure.

The adjusted field pressure forces the play to hit behind the center, just a bit wider than normal because of the pursuit of the nose tackle, who eventually brings down the back after a gain of about four yards.

Ohio State is starting to wear down this defensive line, especially at the point of attack and double teams.

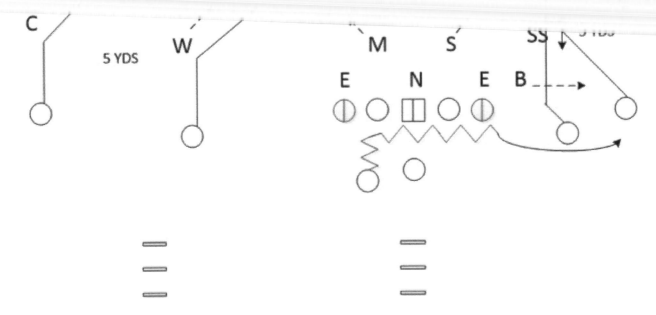

Analysis

Looking to throw the slant side before the ball is even snapped. It looks to be even out on the edge, 2 on 2 out wide to the field, and Cardale's progression reads inside-out. The defense drops the field-side defensive end and Mike linebacker into the slant window for the #2 receiver.

This is the same coverage to the short side of the field that Oregon has used earlier in this game against three receiver sets lined up into the boundary. Once again, the Ducks commit themselves to taking away the short and easy throw.

Ohio State Drive 10 / Play 4 / 1ˢᵗ & 10 / +46 Yard Line / Left Hash / 5:26 3Q
Oregon 20 – OSU 21
Summary
Pass complete to Elliott for a loss of 1 yard

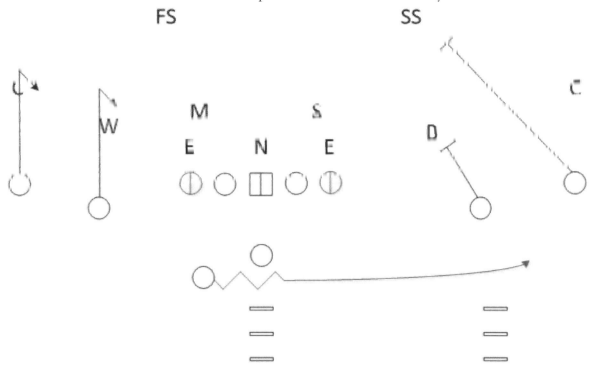

Analysis

With no immediate and obvious chaser from the defense on the motion, Cardale takes the snap and immediately turns and fires into the flat.

The field corner drops to the deep 1/3 but the strong safety rallies to the flat to stop the back for a loss.

The Buckeyes continue to make an effort to get the football out wide, and even though it wasn't really successful this time, the defense has to take the threat seriously because Ohio State has committed themselves to stretching the field in every direction.

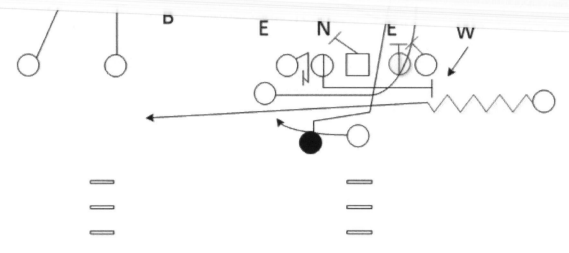

Analysis

Once again the backside inside linebacker over runs the play and doesn't get a proper run fit. The field defensive end chases down the play from behind once again. Right tackle totally missed the block on the backside inside linebacker.

This entire formation is designed to stretch the defense to the field side, and even without a stacked receiver set to the short side of the field, the Will linebacker starts out with a wide alignment that gives plenty of room for running room up inside, and that's exactly where the play hits.

It's good to see the Buckeyes mixup their formations when repeating the same play over and over again.

Ohio State Drive 10 / Play 6 / 3rd & 1 / +37 Yard Line / Right Hash / 4:07 3Q
Oregon 20 – OSU 21

Summary
Elliott runs for a gain of 2 yards and a first down

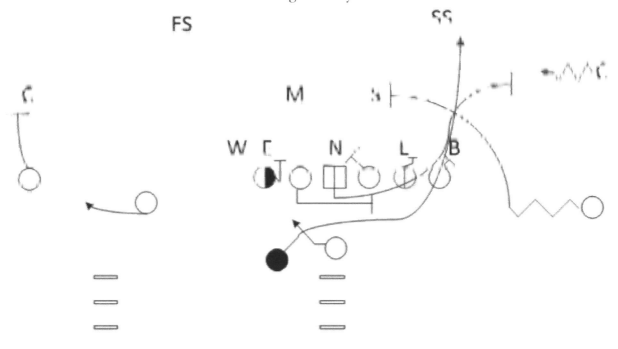

Analysis

The backside defensive end cuts across the face of the left tackle and chases the guard after reading his near foot as he leaves to kick out the other side of the play. The corner to the side of the play does a great job of crack-replace, but is kicked out by the front side guard. Sam shoots the gap and cuts off the path of the left guard. The back still manages to put his head down and get the first down.

Oregon's biggest strength on defense in this game so far has been their ability to shed single blocks and chase plays down from behind, however they've struggled against double-teams and gap schemes, and part of that has to do with their size up front.

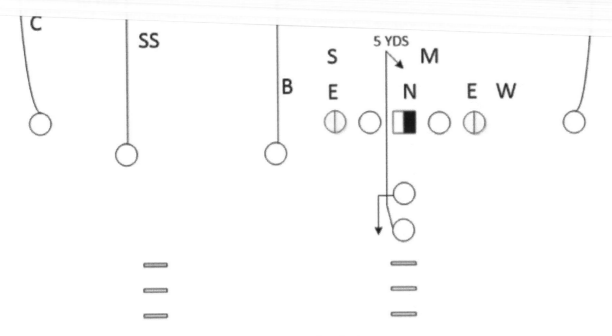

Analysis

Cardale is reading the free safety, eventually checking down the football to the tailback.

This is a simplified version of the four verticals play, but they give the #3 receiver a concrete landmark to turn in and cut across the football field to stretch the coverage.

Oregon once again forces Cardale to check down the football to his last option. By dropping and covering the middle of the field, and creating a great pass rush, the defense doesn't give him a lot of time to scan the field.

<u>Ohio State Drive 10 / Play 8 / 2nd & 3 / +28 Yard Line / Right Hash / 2:56 3Q</u>
Oregon 20 – OSU 21
<u>Summary</u>
Cardale Jones stopped in the backfield for a loss of 1 yard

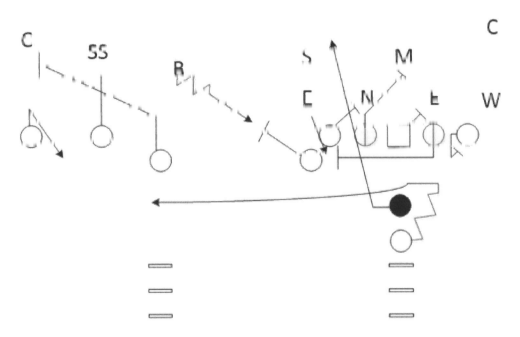

<u>Analysis</u>

The head up 2 technique to the playside beats the double team, which isn't really much of a double team at all, and gets into the backfield to blow up the quarterback run.

Cardale tries to press the hole and does a good job of at least getting back to the line of scrimmage here, which is about the best thing you can say about this play. Cardale is shut down, through no fault of his own, because of a total lack of movement up front.

It would appear that defense is hardly concerned at all with the prospect of a perimeter run or wide throw out of this formation, and are starting to bring pressure to keep the football between the tackles.

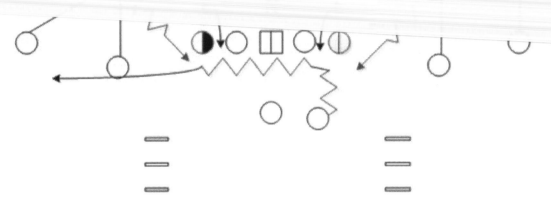

Analysis

Cardale looks toward the double-hitch side of the formation. The edge pressure combined with the drop of the inside linebacker into the hitch window makes it an easy decision to take off and run up the middle and pick up the first down. The defense brings the outside linebacker, edge pressure/ nose drop package that they've been bringing much of the game.

Ohio State Drive 10 / Play 10 / 1st & 10 / +25 Yard Line / Right Hash / 1:44 3Q
Oregon 20 – OSU 21
Summary
Cardale Jones completes the pass to Marshall for a gain of 5 yards

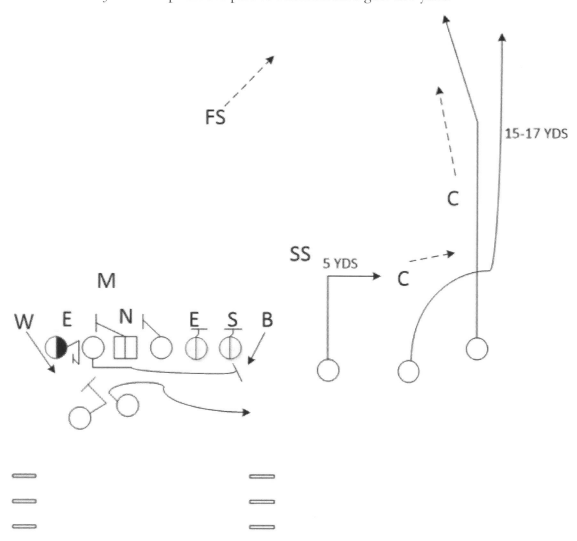

Analysis

It's a normal front seven alignment with man coverage/ corners over, B edge rusher forces Cardale to throw off his back foot but puts it where the receiver can make a great catch.

It's really interesting that this has been one of the most consistent plays for Ohio State in this game, especially considering how much pressure Oregon has brought from the slot, and have put several big hits on the passer as he gets the ball off the slot receiver.

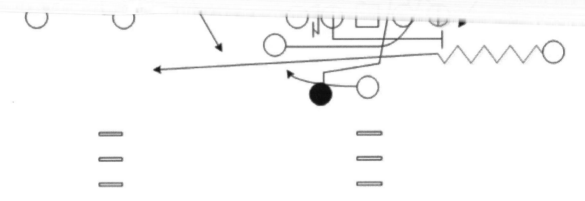

Analysis

Once again the backside inside linebacker does not fit properly, and the back fits right up through the hole, and it's great run blocking, and the only ones who can make the tackle are the guys in the secondary.

Ohio State Drive 10 / Play 12 / 1st & Goal / +10 Yard Line / Middle / 0:32 3Q
Oregon 20 – OSU 21

Summary
Touchdown! Elliott runs for a gain of 10 yards and a score

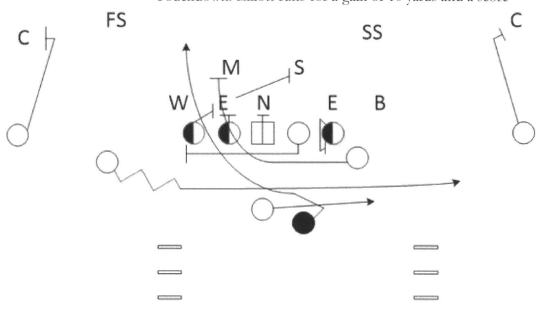

Analysis

The jet motion gets the safety out of position against the counter play, the Will forces the play back inside, and the backside inside linebacker is completely sealed off from the play. It's the easiest run all night, and Ohio State ends the scoring drought.

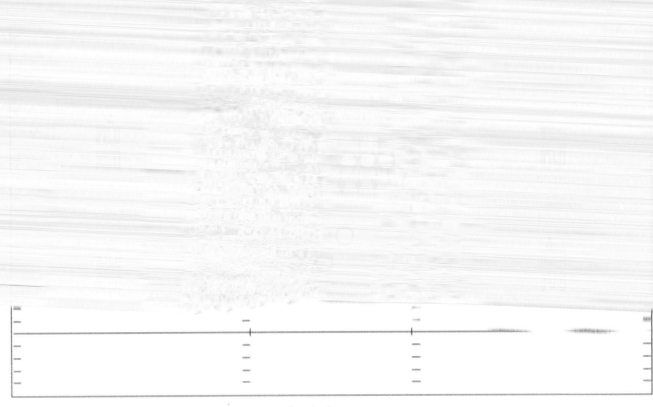

Analysis

Once again, Oregon is coming after the left wing, who is the weak link in the protection.

Ohio State

This drive was a great answ... only a single point. At this p...

All the adjustments and ... drive, with combination of ... most successful, the Buckey...

Oregon

For the Ducks, this was a big letdown. After forcing ... getting the score back to 21-20, there was a lot of confidence o... combination of downhill running and high-percentage passing to impose their will on the defense.

FOLDFOLD

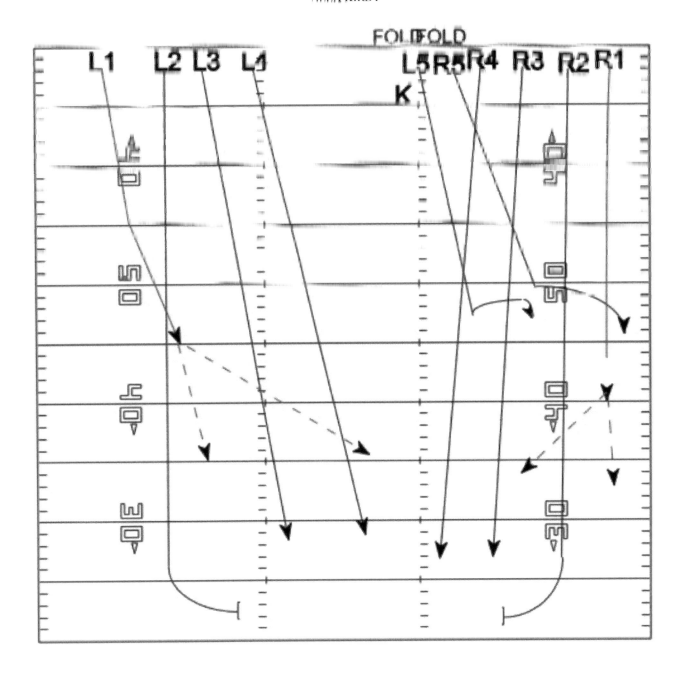

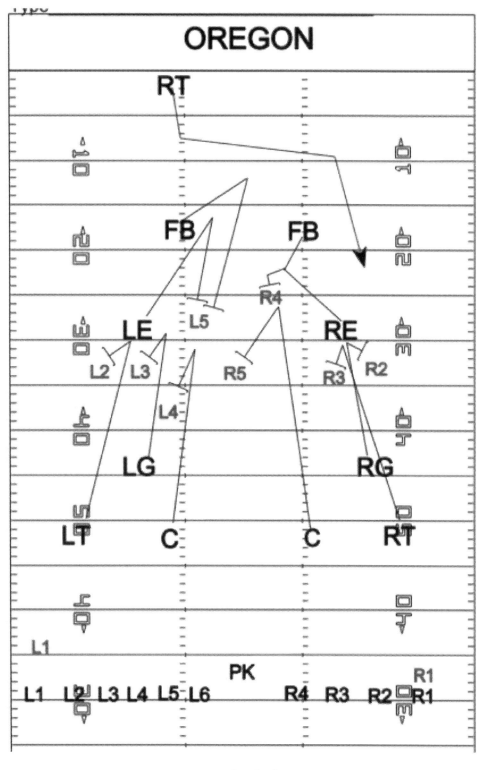

Analysis

The returner should've bounced the ball out to the middle of the field where there's more room.

Oregon Drive 11 / Play 1 / 1ˢᵗ & 10 / -21 / Right Hash / 14:54 4Q
Oregon 20 – Ohio State 28
Summary
Pass complete to Lowe for a gain of 20 yards and a first down

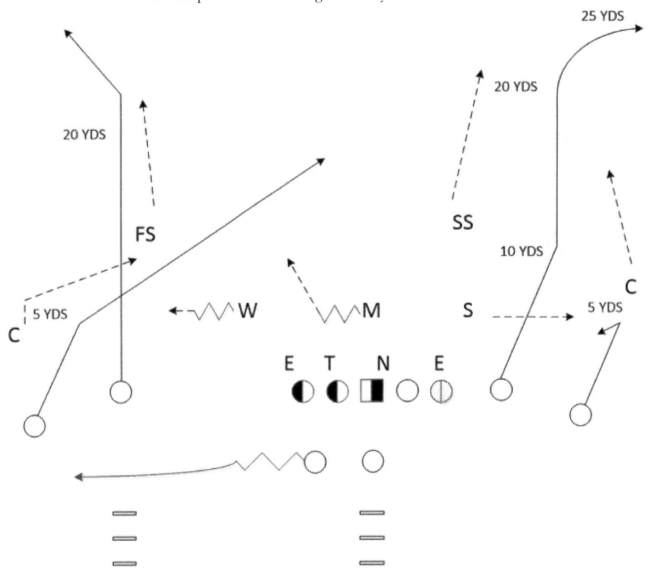

Analysis

Mariota's eyes immediately go to the short side of the field opposite the Mike linebacker once he runs with the motion. However, not only does the defense outnumber the offense in pass coverage, they also have inside leverage on the route concept. He sees the Sam widen and then looks back to toward the left side of the field and the crossing route coming over the middle once the short side of the field is eliminated from the progression. The middle linebacker who is supposed to cut underneath the crossing route steps up over the middle once Mariota steps up in the pocket to avoid the rush, and that creates a passing window for a big gain.

Oregon Drive 11 / Play 2 / 1st & 10 / -41 Yard Line / Right Hash / 14:48 4Q
Oregon 20 – OSU 28
Summary
Freeman runs for no gain

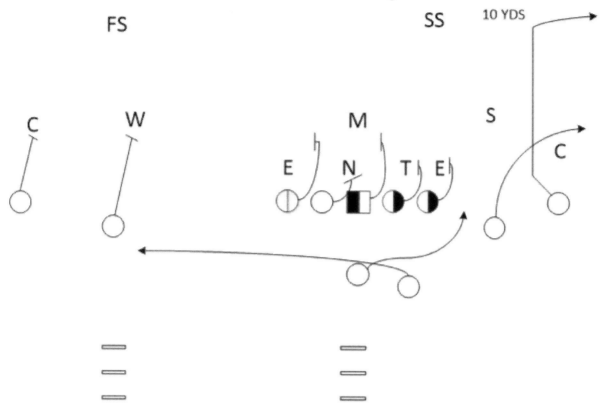

Analysis

Another instance of the inverted zone read that switches up the responsibilities of the QB and the tailback, and can get the ball out on the edge against a defensive end that stays tight to the offensive line.

The slot receiver to the field side is absolutely destroyed by the Will linebacker when trying to block out on the edge.

The QB has a flat-corner concept to the boundary in case he pulls the ball.

Oregon Drive 11 / Play 3 / 2nd & 10 / -41 Yard Line / Left Hash / 14:30 4Q
Oregon 20 – OSU 28
Summary
Incomplete Pass

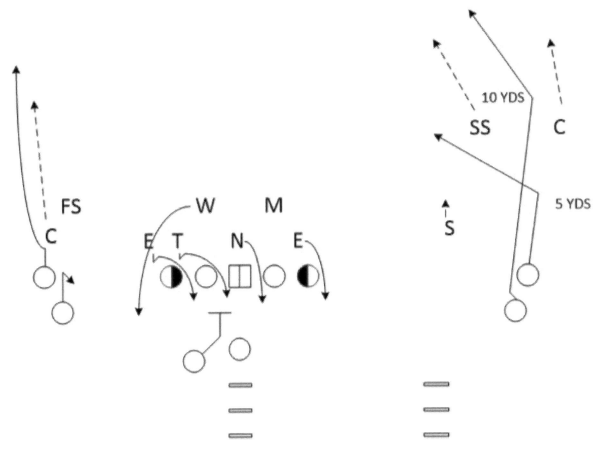

Analysis

Ohio State brought boundary pressure with a stand up defensive end and an outside linebacker.

The FS is aligned just inside of the stacked receiver set to the boundary at about two yards. That by itself should set off some alarm bells in Mariota's head. There is also an edge rusher which should be another key that there's some kind of pressure coming from that side.

The key here is the OLB aligned to the field on the hash who is waiting for the first in-breaking route. He drops straight down the hash, but doesn't have to go far, and undercuts the slant route, getting a hand on it and forcing the incompletion.

This formation forces the defense to declare their intentions.

The wide looping blitz by the boundary linebackers is designed to stop every kind of zone read or QB run scheme to that side of the field.

Oregon Drive 11 / Play 4 / 3rd & 10 / -41 Yard Line / Left Hash / 14:11 4Q
Oregon 20 – OSU 28
Summary
Incomplete pass

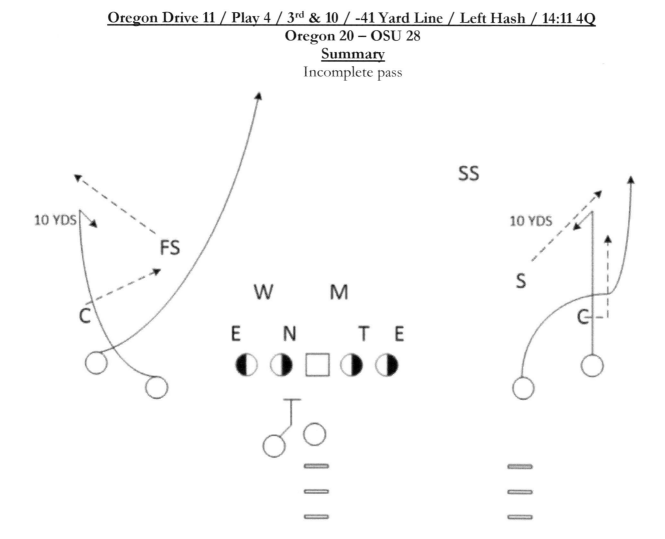

Analysis

The depth of the safeties over #2 to both sides means that on any deep concepts that involve switching of the routes with #1, the defender can easily come over the top and there isn't much chance of a rub/pick that will let one of the receivers loose over the middle.

Mariota is hurried by the rush but manages to get off a decent pass in the area of a wheel route to the wide side of the field. Probably forcing the ball to #9 because he's just locked in to one of the best skill players on the field for Oregon.

If he has more time to throw, he may have been able to reset his feet and find the seam route coming from the short side of the field and away from the rotation of the middle safety.

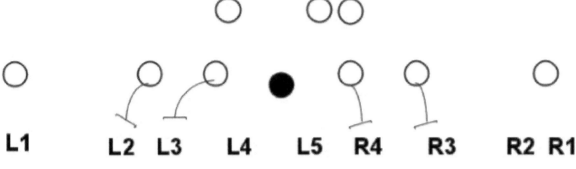

2 MAN SHIELD RT

L1　　L2　L3　　L4　　L5　R4　　R3　　R2 R1

R5

Analysis

The punt protection slides to the boundary in this case because that's where the pressure is coming from. Great call from the middle shield player.

7 MAN
BLOCK

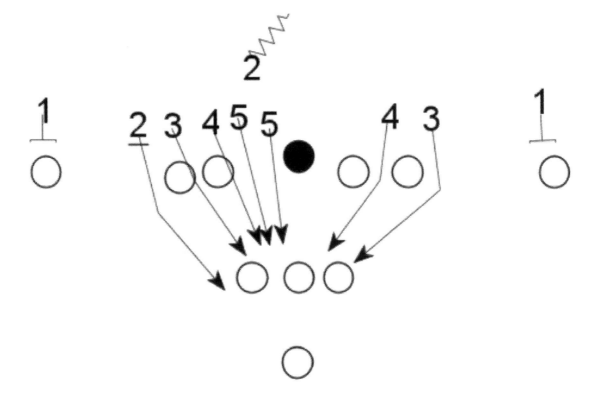

Oregon Drive #11 Review

<u>Oregon</u>

They try to go back to a vertical passing game, but they don't win on first down on the second play of the drive and get behind schedule, which allows Ohio State to get more aggressive and come after the quarterback.

<u>Ohio State</u>

The Buckeye defense gave Oregon some new looks, with pressures coming from the boundary, as well as giving the stacked receiver alignments some extra pressure, with the free safety coming down and playing pretty aggressively against the hitch/fade combination.

Ohio State Drive 11 / Play 1 / 1st & 10 / -24 Yard Line / Left Hash / 13:57 4Q
Oregon 20 – OSU 28
Summary
Marshall runs for a gain of 5 yards

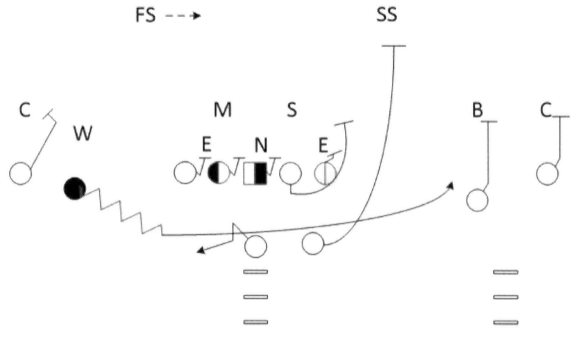

Analysis

The tight end to the field lets his defender cross his face when blocking on the edge, and the blocking back on the edge totally misses the safety going down the field when he ducks his head.

The will linebacker blitzes off the edge once his guy motions into the backfield away from his current position, and ends up playing the cutback.

Also, it's important to remember that Ohio State has been making a living out of this formation by putting a stacked receiver alignment to the boundary, widening the Will linebacker, sending the slot receiver in motion, then running the counter play right back to the boundary. This play keeps the defense on their toes and forces them to account for the possibility of the jet sweep, with the motion man continuing across the formation.

Ohio State Drive 11 / Play 2 / 2nd & 5 / -29 Yard Line / Right Hash / 13:47 4Q
Oregon 20 – OSU 28
Summary
Elliott runs for a gain of 12 yards and a first down

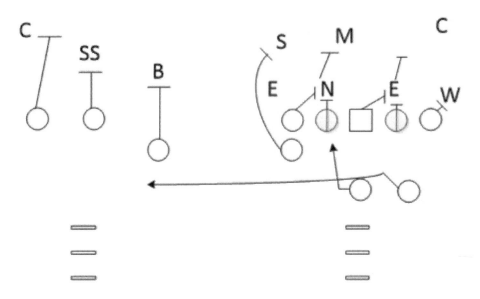

Analysis

The H-back chips the defensive end coming off the line then comes around to seal off the Sam linebacker and creates an alley in between #3 and #4.

The corner, who is unaccounted for in the blocking scheme, chases down the back from behind along with the Mike linebacker who breaks free from the man assigned to him.

At this point, the Oregon defense is struggling to get any movement at all. They're being beaten up the point of attack and haven't had much rest at all since the Oregon offense hasn't been able to stay on the field. The one drive they were able to score lasted a single play, and the defense went right back out on the field after the score.

Ohio State Drive 11 / Play 3 / 1st & 10 / -41 Yard Line / Middle / 13:18 4Q
Oregon 20 – OSU 28
Summary
Pass complete to Thomas for a gain of 23 yards and a first down

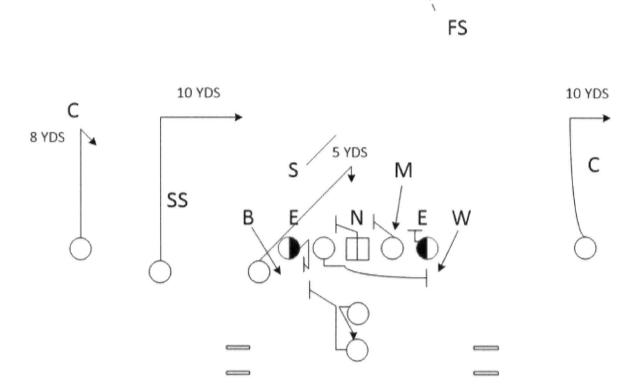

Analysis

Before the snap, Cardale sees that the X receiver singled up on the right side, and at the snap he sees the outside linebacker to that side come off the edge, meaning there is no underneath man to undercut the out route. Cardale gets the ball out as soon as he's done with his playfake.

The progression is set up to be adaptable depending on the pre-snap look. Against the kind of pressure that the defense is bringing here, the 10 yard out is the right call. On the other hand, against a normal look, you could read the progression from left to right.

Even late in the game, Ohio State is pulling out new passing concepts.

Ohio State Drive 11 / Play 4 / 1ˢᵗ & 10 / +36 Yard Line / Right Hash / 12:47 4Q

Oregon 20 – OSU 28

Summary

Smith run for a gain of 3 yards

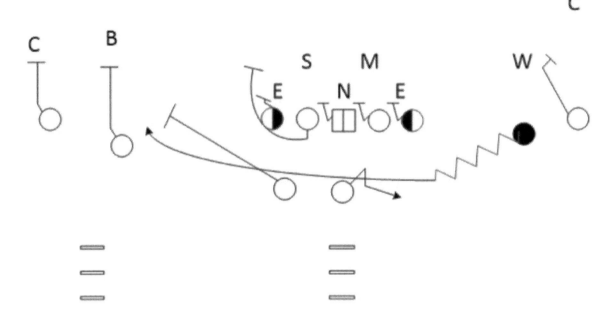

Analysis

Once again we see this offense moving the ball with the perimeter run game, but at the same time creating a reasonable amount of hesitation by giving the defense similar looks to the short side of the field.

The play is designed to hit in the alley between the tackle and the tight end, and the blocking back ends up doubling the outside linebacker with the tight end, and the ball carrier wants to cut back the ball up inside but is tackled by the strong safety because he's unblocked.

Ohio State Drive 11 / Play 5 / 2nd & 7 / +33 Yard Line / Left Hash / 12:16 4Q

Oregon 20 – OSU 28

Summary

Elliott runs for a gain of 2 yards

Analysis

This play can hit anywhere from inside the right offensive tackle, to all the way out on the perimeter depending on who's carrying the football and what the blocking scheme looks like once the ball is snapped.

In this case, the back gets to the edge so quickly that the H-back can't get any real block on the blitzer. The defensive end ends up making the tackle on the edge because the outside linebacker to the field is right behind the ball carrier, and there is no room out on the edge to cut it around to the sideline because the defensive backs are forcing the ball back inside.

The reason the ball is given to the tailback out on the edge is because of the slant by the defensive end on the outside shoulder of the right tackle, as he comes inside and closes the open space in the interior, the quarterback's rad is to hand the ball off to the back let him loose on the edge.

Ohio State Drive 11 / Play 6 / 3ʳᵈ & 5 / +31 Yard Line / Right Hash / 11:43 4Q
Oregon 20 – OSU 28
Summary
Pass complete to Marshall for a gain of 19 yards and a first down

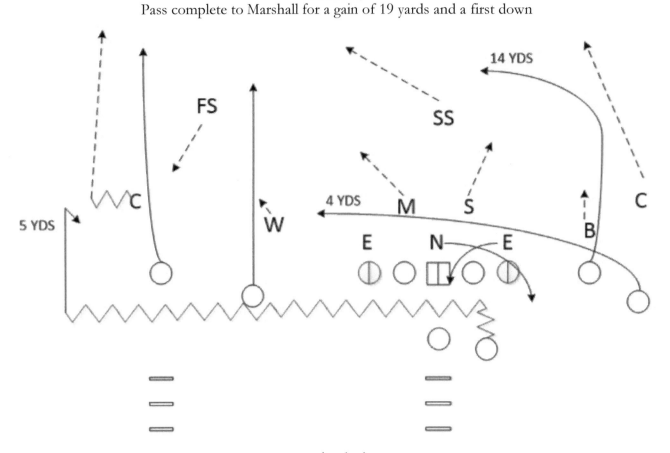

Analysis

Cardale is locked in on the drive concept to the right side of the field, never even considers the wide side of the field. Since the drive route is covered by all the underneath defenders, he immediately starts staring down the basic cross route that comes open late over the middle.

The reason the offense motions the back out so far is to take the corner out of the equation. Normally, when a receiver runs a hitch route to the outside and he's within a reasonable distance of another receiver running a route, the corner keeps dropping and opens up to expect some kind of hi/lo route, similar to how the defense played the smash route on the 2nd drive of the game. This also means that the flat defender can't get out wide enough to play the underneath route so that the corner can commit to playing the top of the smash concept.

In this example the corner squats down on the hitch route and the free safety collisions the #2 receiver going vertical but lets him go to play the flat, assuming that the corner will squeeze and split the difference between #1 and #2, but instead the #2 vertical is wide open on the goal line.

Ohio State Drive 11 / Play 7 / 1st & 10 / +12 Yard Line / Middle / 11:09 4Q
Oregon 20 – OSU 28
Summary
Samuel run for a gain of 6 yards

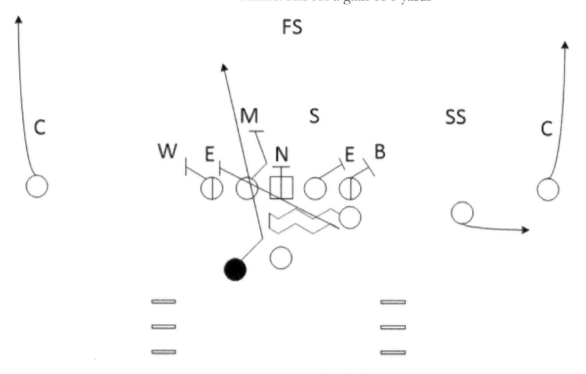

Analysis

The backside inside linebacker ends up making the tackle because there is no real mess at the point of attack in the middle of the play like usual in this instance. The hope is that the misdirection in the backfield will freeze the Sam linebacker in his place, but since the defense has seen this play several times already, the Sam linebacker ends up making the tackle.

I hate the decision to cut the defensive end here, because the end result is that any open space on either side of the block is now cluttered up with both players bodies on the ground, eliminating any chance of squeezing through any creases in the middle of the defense. The end does a great job of eliminating any open space and forcing such a tight fit to begin with.

Ohio State Drive 11 / Play 8 / 2nd & 4 / +6 Yard Line / Left Hash / 10:29 4Q
Oregon 20 – OSU 28

Summary
Elliott runs for a gain of 4 yards and a first down

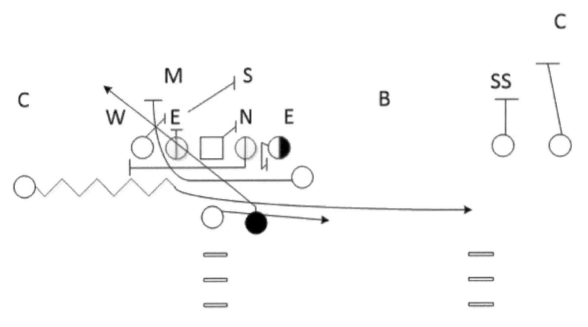

Analysis

Against a normal zone scheme, the offensive line is sliding away from the back, and the tight end is left one-on-one with the defensive end. This way the defensive end's slanting away from the edge defenders gets blocked out on by the front side combo block from the right tackle and the tight end.

The offensive line is moving toward the field and the back is aligned toward the direction of the play. The defense sells out against the run, and the safeties are aligned over the slot receivers.

The read for the back is the same, only he's starting out on the opposite side of the play since the OL is moving toward the back instead of away from him.

The back hits the front side of the play, and with both of the linebackers to that side of the formation outside the tight end, there's no one at the second level in the B gap to stop the pile from spilling into the end zone.

Ohio State Drive 11 / Play 9 / +2 Yard Line / Left Hash / 9:57 4Q
Oregon 20 – OSU 28
Summary
Touchdown! Elliott runs for a gain of 2 yards and a score

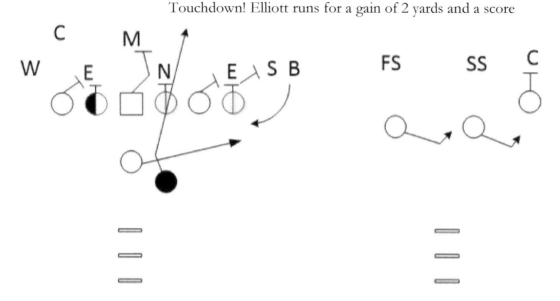

Analysis

Against a normal zone scheme, the offensive line is sliding away from the back, and the tight end is left one-on-one with the defensive end. This way the defensive end's slanting away from the edge defenders gets blocked out on by the front side combo block from the right tackle and the tight end.

The offensive line is moving toward the field and the back is aligned toward the direction of the play. The defense sells out against the run, and the safeties are aligned over the slot receivers.

The read for the back is the same, only he's starting out on the opposite side of the play since the OL is moving toward the back instead of away from him.

The back hits the frontside of the play, and with both of the linebackers to that side of the formation outside the tight end, there's no one at the second level in the B gap to stop the pile from spilling into the end zone.

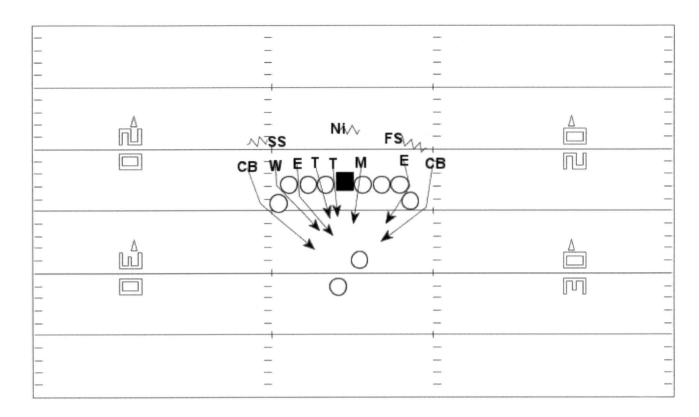

Analysis

Interesting that Ohio State switches the wings, so that they can put the better of the two wing blockers on the left side to deal with the constant pressure on that side. However, the Oregon field goal block team sets their strength based on #48, who is now lined up on the right side of the formation, so all that really happens is the strength of the field goal block team comes off the right side.

Ohio State Drive #11 Review

<u>Ohio State</u>

· For the most part, the Buckeyes have settled on a successful group of formations, with the unbalanced receiver sets and 2x2 formation with stacked receiver sets into the short side of the field.

· Ohio State has found a way to use one-back sets to run two-back run schemes.

<u>Oregon</u>

· The defense is out of adjustments at this point, and the players are completely gassed.

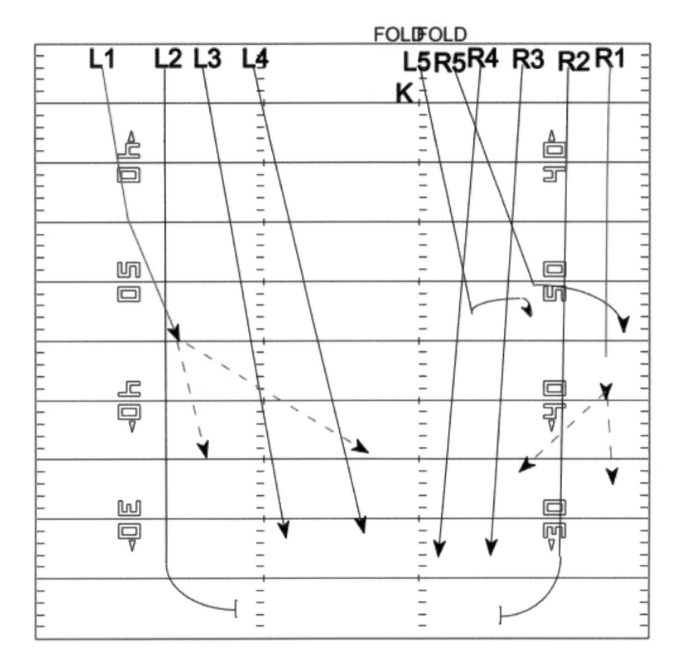

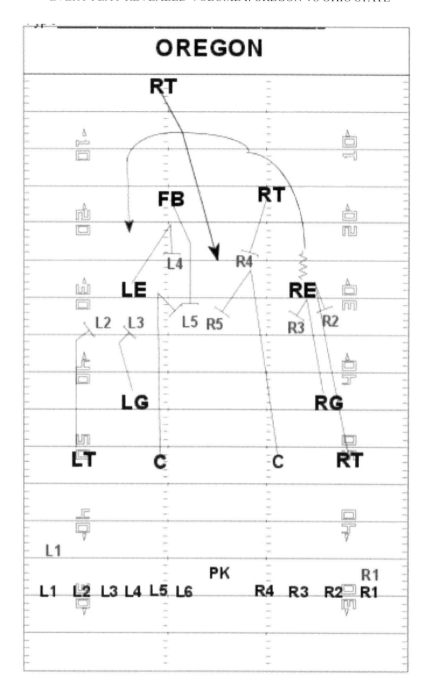

Analysis

Oregon runs a fake reverse on the return scheme. They line up #9 at the right end position, who usually doesn't line up there. As a result he lends more weight to the fake reverse and creates a crease to run up the middle.

Oregon Drive 12 / Play 1 / 1ˢᵗ & 10 / -10 Yard Line / Right Hash / 9:32 4Q
Oregon 20 – OSU 35
Summary
Pass complete to Baylis for a gain of 9 yards

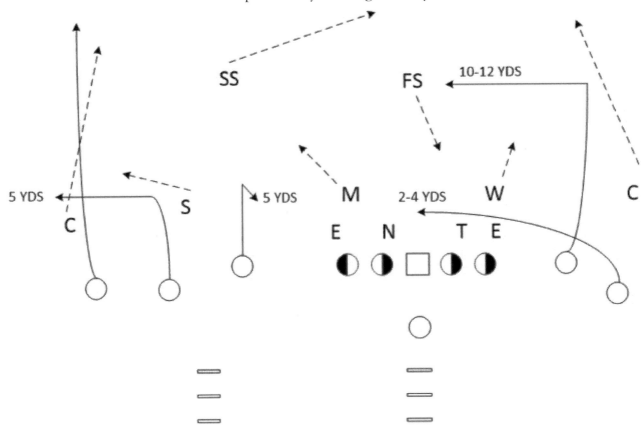

Analysis

It's 3 on 3 underneath to the field side, and the stick is wide open because the Mike linebacker doesn't get over in time. Notice the alignment of the Mike is only a yard or two further inside than the last time Oregon lined up in Empty with the stick concept in this part of the field, and that small difference makes all the difference in the world, since Mariota is still throwing off of the Mike's alignment and drop. This also tells the Y to run a simple in-breaking hitch route.

The safety comes down underneath to the boundary to take away the QB run and crowd up the middle of the field.

Oregon Drive 12 / Play 2 / 2ⁿᵈ & 6 / -14 Yard Line / Left Hash / 9:08 4Q
Oregon 20 – OSU 35
Summary
Tyner runs for a gain of 9 yards and a first down

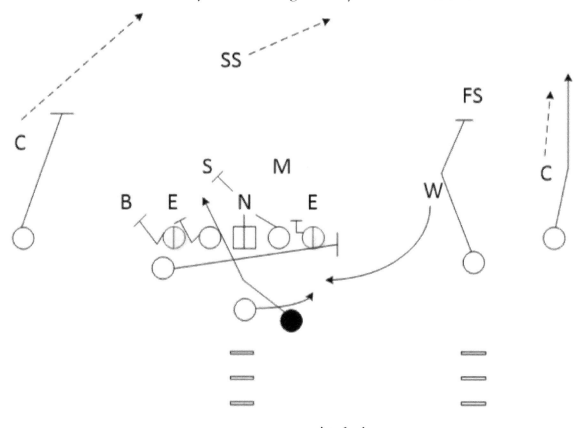

Analysis

(This play comes after a false start penalty that backed the offense up 5 yards)

The TE coming across the formation coupled with the extremely wide path of the OL coming the other direction holds the linebackers in place.

The cutback hole opens up right up the middle because the back's first and second reads are both pushed to the sideline. The guy who makes the tackle (Mike) is the scraper who had to fill the C gap and replace the DE to play the QB, then redirect to chase him down from behind.

Defense comes with pressure from the outside linebacker position at the wide side of the field, and the TE coming across cuts off the path of the blitzer.

This is one of the rare times that Oregon attempts to run the stretch play, and uses the numbers advantage to the short side of the field to create a crease up the middle, and they're able to pick up the first down.

Oregon Drive 12 / Play 3 / 1ˢᵗ & 10 / -23 Yard Line / Left Hash / 8:50 4Q
Oregon 20 – OSU 35
Summary
Incomplete pass

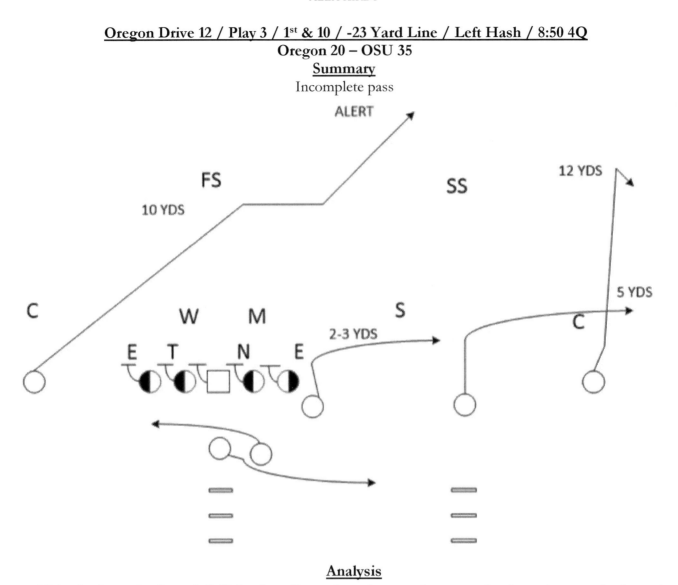

Analysis

This play is on the "speed dial" for the offense since they ran the same play from the same hash on the first drive in a hurry up scenario after picking up a first down.

The defense stays in their base look with a downhill safety to the 3 receiver side.

Mariota is knocked out for a play when he rolls out to the right, and after the whistle the players get in a fight, resulting in a 15 yard personal foul penalty against Oregon.

Oregon Drive 12 / Play 4 / 2ⁿᵈ & 26 / -7 Yard Line / Left Hash / 8:36 4Q
Oregon 20 – OSU 35
Summary
Incomplete pass

Analysis

The backup QB is in for this play. It says a lot about both the urgency of the situation and Oregon's faith in their backup QB to go empty inside of their own –10 yard line.

The defensive line doesn't have to play as disciplined, and they force the QB out of the pocket. The Mike comes down to force a bad throw as the QB rolls out to the right and tries to throw the drive route coming over the middle to the right flat.

Not much you could hope for in this situation, this guy hasn't seen any significant action all season.

Oregon Drive 12 / Play 5 / 3rd & 26 / -7 Yard Line / Left Hash / 8:28 4Q
Oregon 20 – OSU 35
Summary
Pass complete to Stanford for a gain of 19 yards

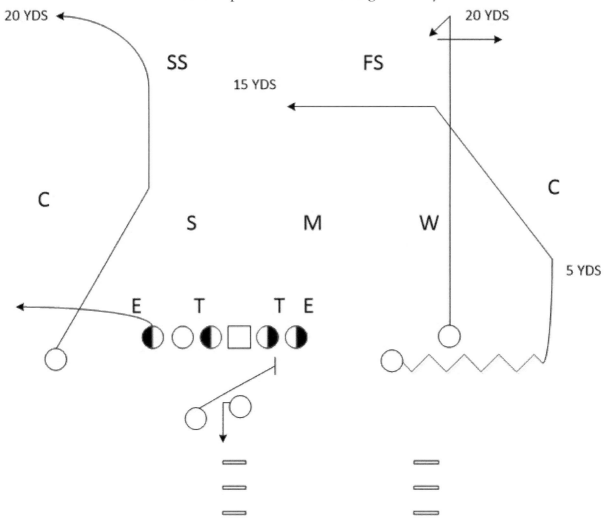

Analysis

Mariota comes back on the field for this play on 3rd and forever.

The man running the dig route brings the safety and the linebackers with him, opening up the deep curl/pivot route, and this is a good throw to get the ball into that window. Mariota doesn't even try the boundary side of the concept, the deep out to the opposite side is an outlet.

It's a good throw, but it's still not enough to pick up the first down.

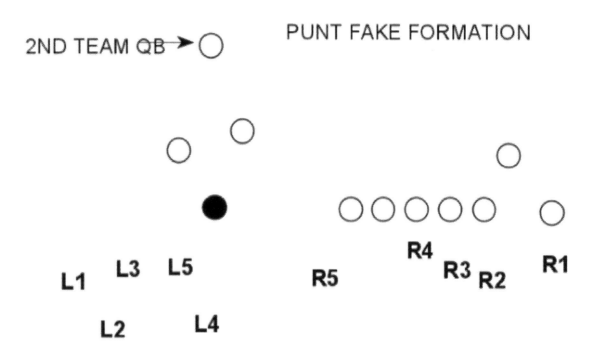

2ND TEAM QB

PUNT FAKE FORMATION

R4

R5   R3 R2   R1

L3 L5

L1

L2   L4

Analysis

Oregon makes Ohio State burn a timeout when they line up with a polecat formation and the backup quarterback is in a position to take the snap and likely throw a pass.

2 MAN SHIELD RT

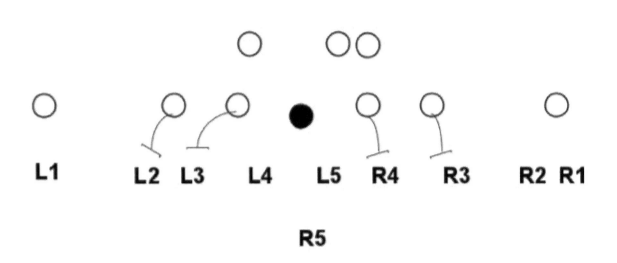

SAFE RET

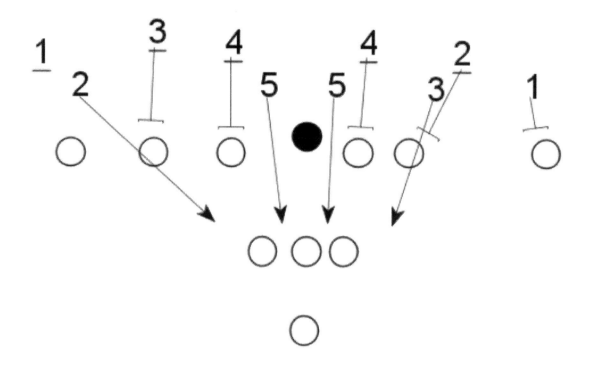

Oregon Drive #12 Review

Oregon

A promising drive stalled because of mistakes, a momentary injury, and penalties. If it had been 4th and 5 instead of 4th and 26, it's likely Oregon would've tried for the 1st down, but other than a trick play attempt on the fake punt formation, there's no chance they line up normally and attempt to pick up the 1st down.

Ohio State

The Buckeyes get lucky when Oregon makes a dumb mistake and puts themselves in a 2nd and 26 and the offense has basically no chances of success on the drive.

Ohio State Drive 12 / Play 1 / 1st & 10 / -39 Yard Line / Left Hash / 7:40 4Q
Oregon 20 – OSU 35
Summary
Elliott runs for a 3 yard gain

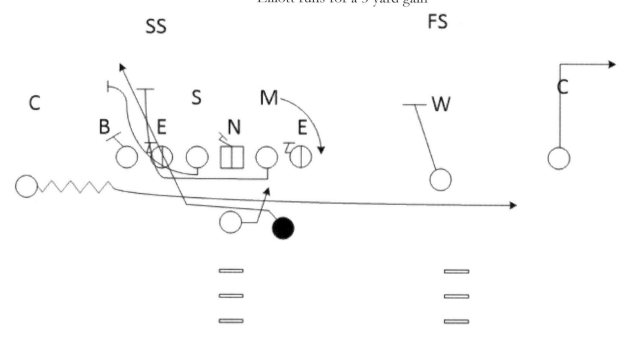

Analysis

Ohio State is hoping to manufacture a big play by removing the safeties from the equation. The corner is right there, and the offense loses their crack-back block guy when they motion him instead.

However this motion accomplishes something similar to the crack back block. By creating hesitation and misdirection at the point of attack, he eliminates the aggressiveness of the defenders to the front side of the play, and makes it that much easier for the offensive line to locate and block them.

Ohio State Drive 12 / Play 2 / 2nd & 7 / -42 Yard Line / Left Hash / 7:26 4Q
Oregon 20 – OSU 35
Summary
Elliott runs for a gain of 8 yards and a first down

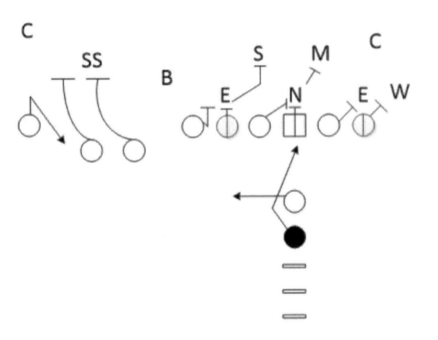

Analysis

The back gets skinny and finds a crease inside. Once again the corner makes the tackle. The offensive line does a great job of pushing the defensive line to the side and coming off of combos to the next level.

Another inside zone play ran out of an unbalanced formation lined up into the boundary.

Ohio State Drive 12 / Play 3 / 1st & 10 / 50 Yard Line / Left Hash / 7:00 4Q
Oregon 20 – OSU
Summary
Elliott runs for no gain

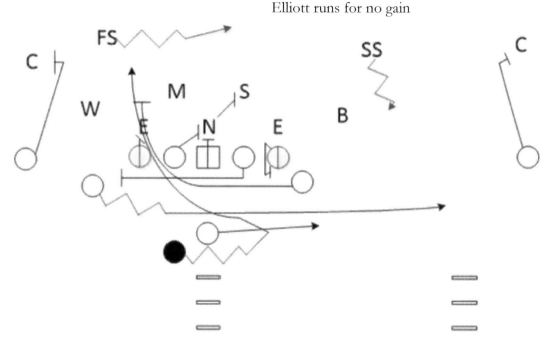

Analysis

The front side guard gets slowed down in the hole, which dooms the play to failure. The offensive line fails to create any movement or running room to the open side, mainly because the offense plays as aggressively downhill at the point of attack and the pullers lose all their momentum and the timing is all screwed up.

The offense continues to attempt to move the ball by taking advantage of the numerical advantage and open spaces to the short side of the field. Hesitation is a big part of why this play fails, since the front side guard would be better off blocking the wrong guy at full speed than blocking no one and stopping their feet at the point of attack.

Ohio State Drive 12 / Play 4 / 2nd & 10 / 50 Yard Line / Left Hash / 6:22 4Q
Oregon 20 – OSU 35
Summary
Elliott runs for a gain of 3 yards

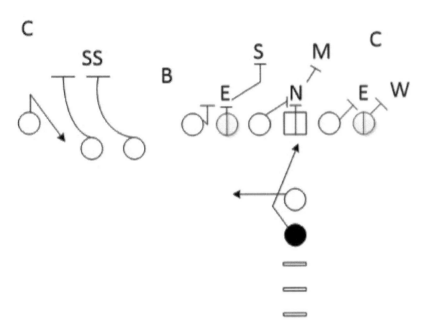

Analysis

The overhang defender (B) forces the ball carrier to cutback inside, where the nose does a great job holding his ground against the double team, so there is no real running room.

Still, they actually do a good job of picking up yardage on this play and staying positive.

The defensive end working against the right guard first holds up the B gap, forcing the guard on his heels, then allowing him to come across the guard's face and help on the tackle.

Ohio State Drive 12 / Play 5 / 3ʳᵈ & 7 / +47 Yard Line / Left Hash / 5:44 4Q
Oregon 20 – OSU 35
Summary
Cardale Jones runs for a gain of 6 yards

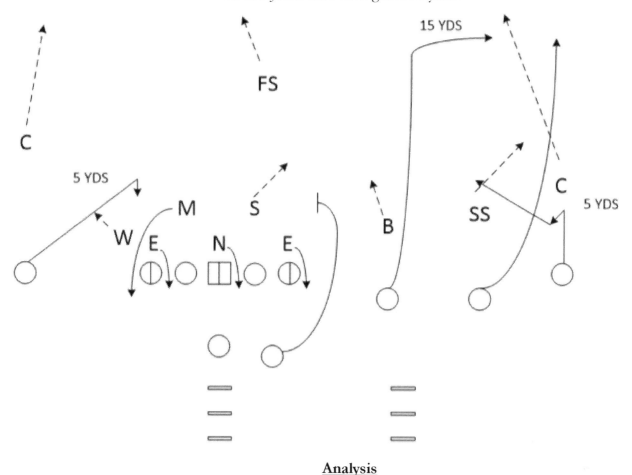

Analysis

This play looks like a downfield pass play, but is in fact a uniquely designed QB draw where the tail back in the backfield is supposed to force the inside linebackers to widen and clear out the middle .

No one on offense is running their pass routes with much precision or urgency, so the defense is never threatened much on the edge.

Cardale is at his best in these situations, when the offensive line provides a wide birth, and gives him plenty of room to operate up the middle.

RUGBY PUNT

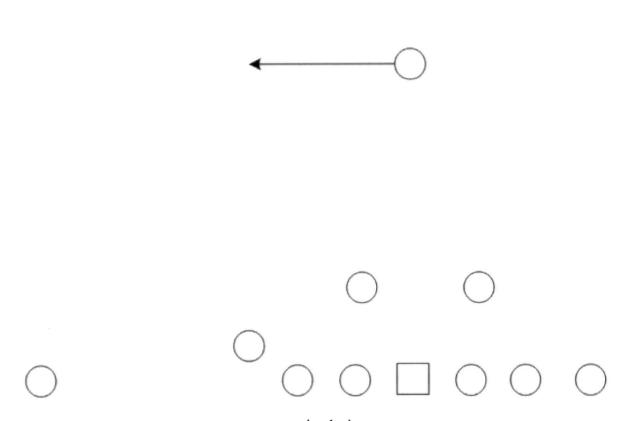

<u>Analysis</u>

Ohio State brings in #2 off the hip of the tackle to provide some extra blocking on the edge, as they know they'll be facing plenty of pressure at this point in the game.

OHIO STATE PUNT RETURN FORMATIONS

SAFE RET

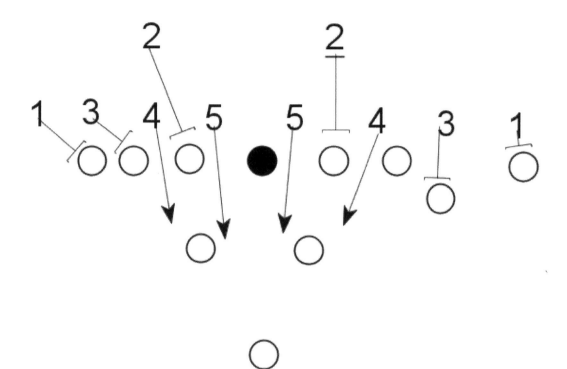

Ohio State Drive #12 Review

Ohio State

The Buckeyes keep it on the ground during the entire drive, and it's clear that they have no intention of putting the football in the air, even on 3rd and long. The focus here is on playing very conservative, taking advantage of field position, the clock, and the 15 point cushion they have on the scoreboard. Ohio State's success in moving the football across the 50 yard line makes it an easy decision to put the football and pin Oregon deep inside their own 20 yard line.

Oregon

Once again this defense gives the offense an opportunity, but the Ducks are on their last gasp, and will need to go the length of the field twice in order to tie the game.

Oregon Drive 13 / Play 1 / 1st & 10 / -15 Yard Line / Left Hash / 4:17 4Q
Oregon 20 – OSU 35
Summary

Pass complete to Stanford for a gain of 29 yards, but called back for offensive holding

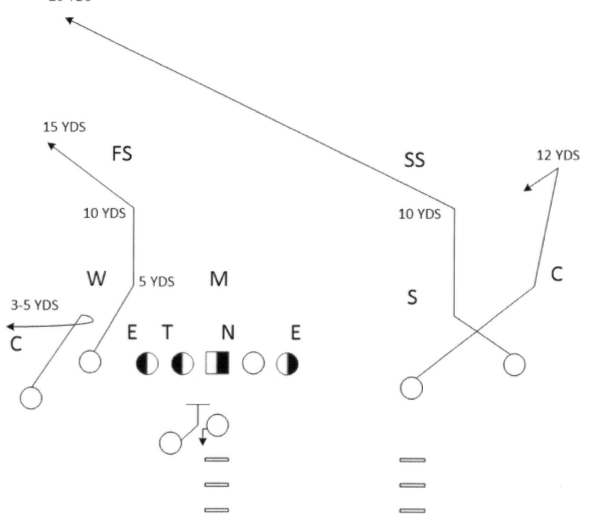

Analysis

The smash concept to the boundary side accomplishes the same as a clear-out route going vertical in the classic deep cross concept. The corner route occupies the safety, but he stays as a viable receiving options, and allows the deep crosser to come over the top late with no defenders in that area except the defender trailing behind him.

Mariota is flushed out and it messes up the timing on the throw.

Oregon Drive 13 / Play 2 / 1ˢᵗ & 17 / -8 Yard Line / Left Hash / 4:07 4Q
Oregon 20 – OSU 35
<u>**Summary**</u>
Mariota runs for a gain of 7 yards

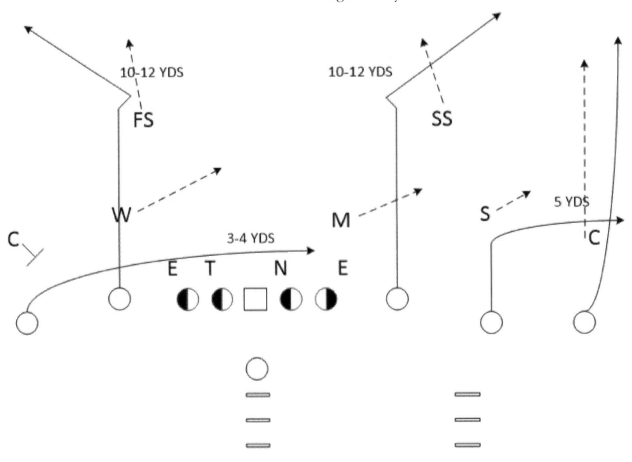

<u>**Analysis**</u>

The defense has to play 4 on 3 and 3 on 2 on either side of the formation, meaning that there aren't any linebackers left to sit over the middle until the Will passes off the drive route to the Mike, then Mariota takes off on the scramble.

The defense is playing a combination coverage with a pressed corner and a safety playing the deep half to the boundary, while the secondary to the wide side of the field plays a cover 4 scheme.

Oregon Drive 13 / Play 3 / 2ⁿᵈ & 10 / -15 Yard Line / Right Hash / 3:50 4Q
Oregon 20 – OSU 35
Summary
Pass complete to Tyner for a loss of one yard

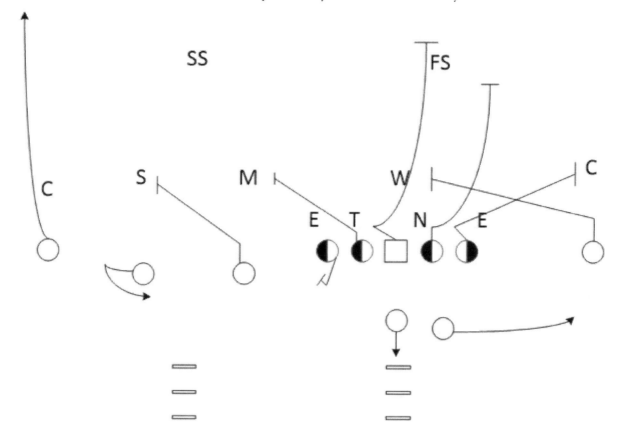

Analysis

This is why I don't like throwing a tailback screen into a hard corner to the boundary. Mariota gets locked into the tailback side of the screen because the defense didn't declare decisively to the tailback side of the play. The corner was way too fast for the RT to get out on the edge to seal off the corner from the play.

The defense had been playing a hard corner to the boundary against 3x1 sets for much of the game.

After the offense gets back to the original line of scrimmage, they try to take advantage of the aggressive pass rush from Ohio State.

<u>Oregon Drive 13 / Play 4 / 3rd & 11 / -14 Yard Line / Right Hash / 3:18 4Q</u>
Oregon 20 – OSU 35
<u>Summary</u>
Incomplete pass

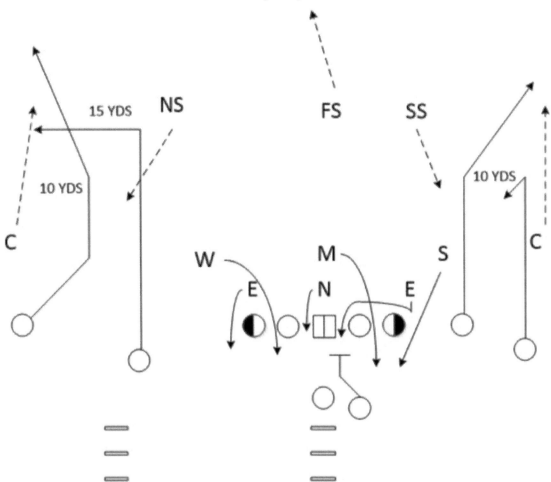

<u>Analysis</u>

When under pressure, most QBs revert to his habits and what he's most comfortable with. The defense knows this, and you can see the FS shaded toward the boundary, dropping on the right hash. The corner on the boundary side is also anticipating some kind of underneath route, and jumps on the receiver in front of him once he sees the hitch route develop.

Oregon Drive 13 / Play 5 / 4th & 11 / -14 Yard Line / Right Hash / 2:53 4Q
Oregon 20 – OSU 25
Summary
Incomplete pass

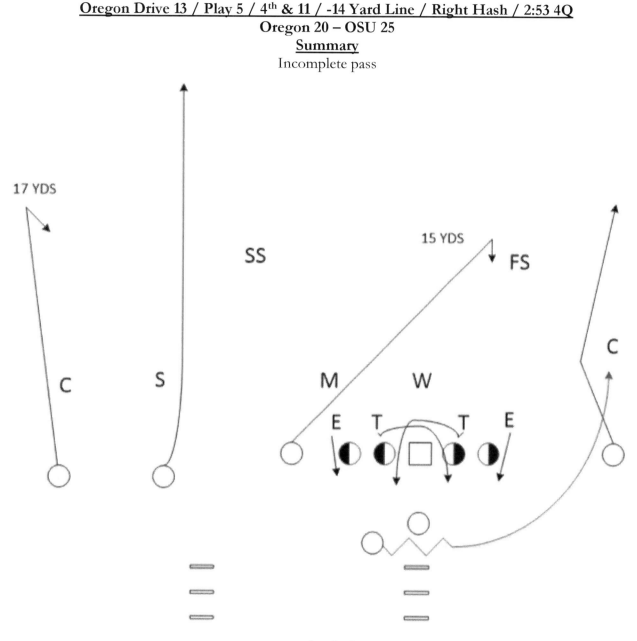

Analysis

Mariota originally looks to the middle of the field expecting the combination of the seam route and the deep sit down by the TE to stretch the middle of the field and put the safeties in conflict. This is similar to the play Oregon used in the third quarter to score a touchdown in one play after an Ohio State turnover.

The play is timed up so that Mariota should look to the sideline for the X receiver in the hole between the corner and the safety, but the throw is too late. Mariota spent too much time waiting for a throw over the middle to come open and ended up making the right read but waited too long.

Oregon Drive #13 Review

Oregon

Oregon is grasping for straws on this drive, their backs are against the wall. The stop on 4th down pretty much seals it, and hands the ball back to Ohio State in prime field position.

Ohio State

Surprised that Ohio State brought pressure on that 3rd and long after holding back and playing coverage for a while on the last couple of drives.

Ohio State Drive 13 / Play 1 / 1st & 10 / +14 Yard Line / Left Hash / 2:45 4Q
Oregon 20 – OSU 35
Summary
Cardale Jones runs for a gain of 2 yards

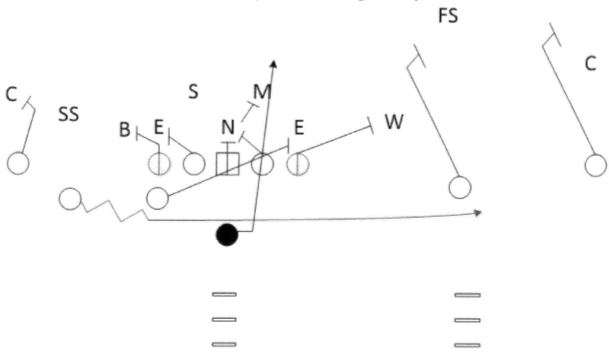

Analysis
The backside inside linebacker makes the tackle after coming over the top of the combo.

This play requires the ability to get skinny and vertical in a hurry. You can't cut it back because is no blocking to the backside. Still, there isn't much of a hole to the front side either. The motion brings the safety into the box, eight defenders vs five blockers is a bad equation.

It's a creative idea, but given the inconsistent running ability of Cardale between the tackles, there are definitely better and more proven ways to move the football when you're trying to eat up clock and put the final nail in the coffin.

Ohio State Drive 13 / Play 2 / 2nd & 8 / +12 Yard Line / Left Hash / 2:35 4Q
Oregon 20 – OSU 35
Summary
Elliott runs for a gain of 5 yards

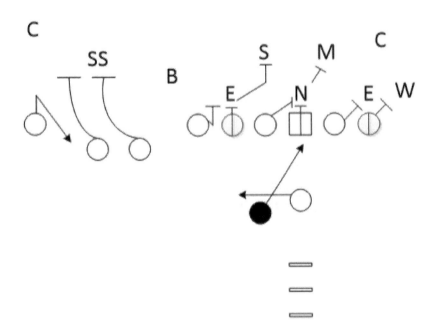

Summary
The Sam shoots the gap, but the RT has his eyes up and pushes him out of the play. The defensive end on the opposite side of the play, and the "B" linebacker made the tackle after a good gain.

The defense isn't concerned at all with the possibility of the throw to the hitch screen.

Ohio State Drive 13 / Play 3 / 3rd & 3 / +7 Yard Line / Left Hash / 2:17 4Q
Oregon 20 – OSU 35
Summary
Elliott runs for a gain of 2 yards

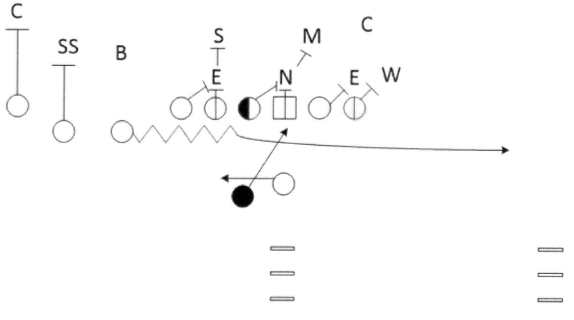

Analysis
The offense is lining up once again and running inside zone.

I don't like adding motion to the play because it doesn't solve the biggest problem of getting movement up front, and it brings more defenders to the play, the outside linebacker and the free safety. The backside inside linebacker chases the motion, but there isn't enough movement on the front side, and the nose is pushed over but occupies the center and the left guard and forces the ball carrier to stay skinny and the B rushes around the edge.

Ohio State Drive 13 / Play 4 / 4th & 1 / +4 Yard Line / Left Hash / 1:47 4Q
Oregon 20 – OSU 35
Summary
Ohio State draws Oregon offsides with the hardcount

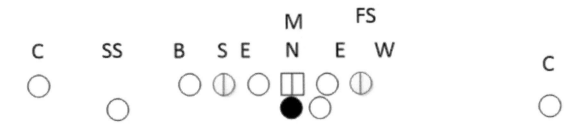

Ohio State Drive 13 / Play 5 / 1st & Goal / +2 Yard Line / Left Hash / 1:43 4Q
Oregon 20 – OSU 35
Summary
Elliott runs for a gain of 1 yard

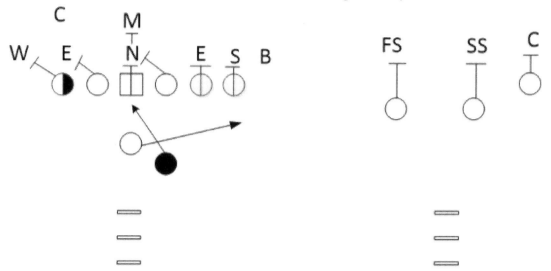

Analysis

The edge rusher makes sure there isn't a front side running lane. The 4i technique disrupts the combo on the nose which opens up the gap for the Mike, who drags the ball carrier down from behind and keeps him out of the end zone.

There's a problem to the open side, getting a 3 on 2 including the corner, and the guard coming off the combo takes the corner, the defensive end slants inside into the open gap, and that creates the room on the edge for the back.

Should've been a touchdown.

<u>Ohio State Drive 13 / Play 6 / 2nd & Goal / +1 Yard Line / Left Hash / 1:07 4Q</u>
Oregon 20 – OSU 35
<u>Summary</u>
Touchdown! Elliot runs for a gain of 1 yard and a score.

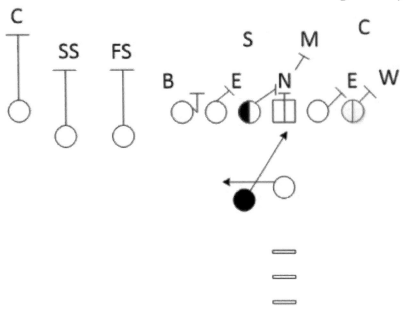

<u>Analysis</u>
Cardale checks to change the tight end's block to block out on the outside linebacker, and the Sam isn't touched but it's so close to the end zone that the back's momentum takes him across the goal line. If the tight end doesn't block out, the play will be forced to cutback right into the strong outside linebacker.

It's a touchdown, and the Ohio State sideline starts to celebrate.

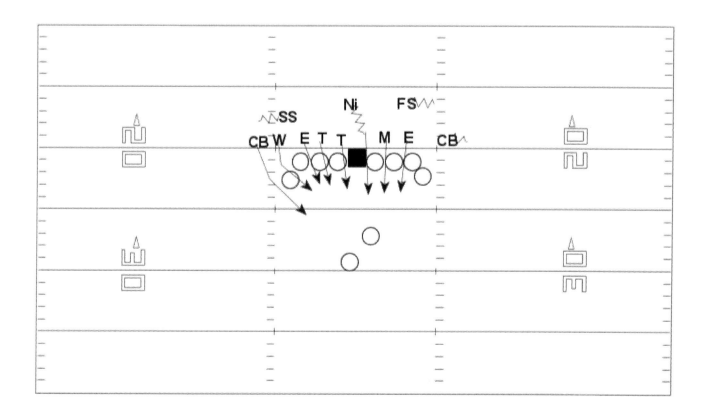

Ohio State Drive #13 Review

Ohio State

This final drive was the one that put the nail in the coffin. Using unbalanced formations and straight-ahead, downhill running plays, the Buckeyes imposed their will on a tired and beaten Oregon defense. The final score of the night sealed the victory and the National Championship for Ohio State.

Oregon

Despite completely selling out against the run, there wasn't much Oregon could do to stop Ohio State on this final drive.

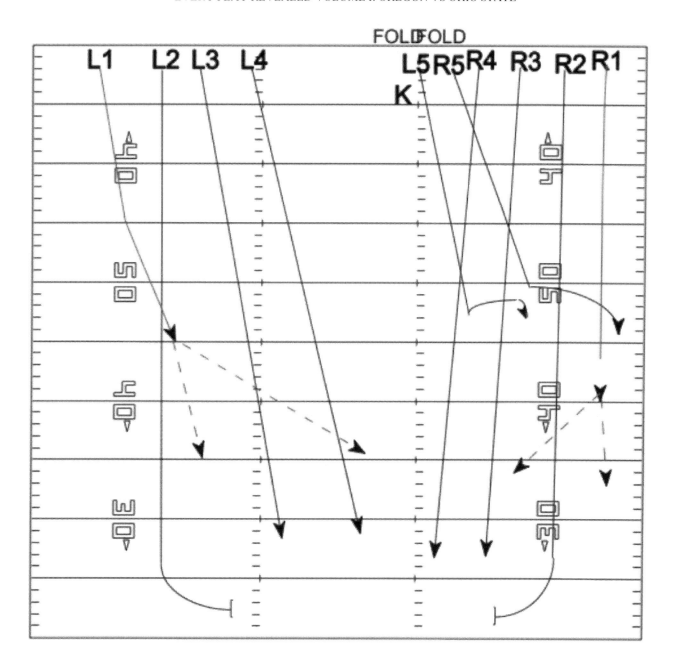

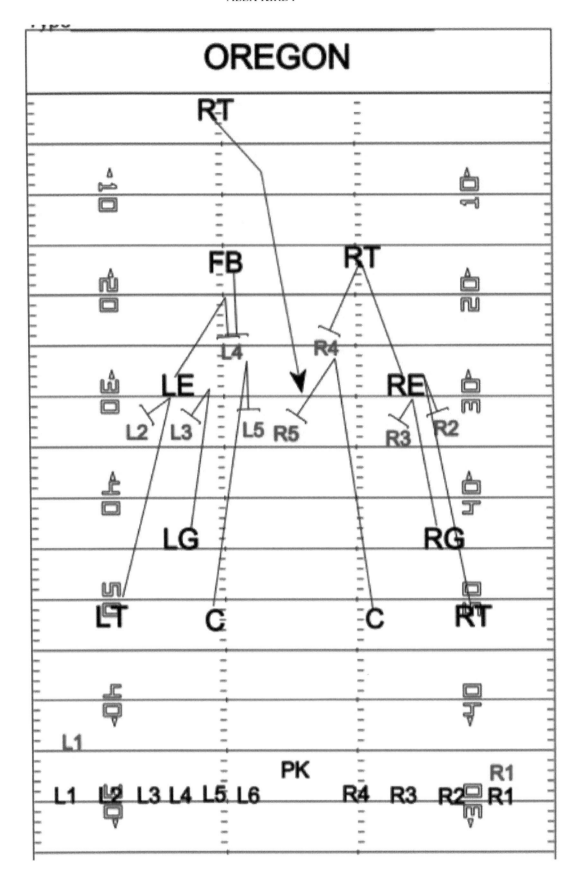

Oregon Drive 14 / Play 1 / 1ˢᵗ & 10 / -20 Yard Line / Right Hash / 0:27 4Q
Oregon 20 – OSU 42
Summary
Pass complete to Marshall for a gain of 23 yards and a first down

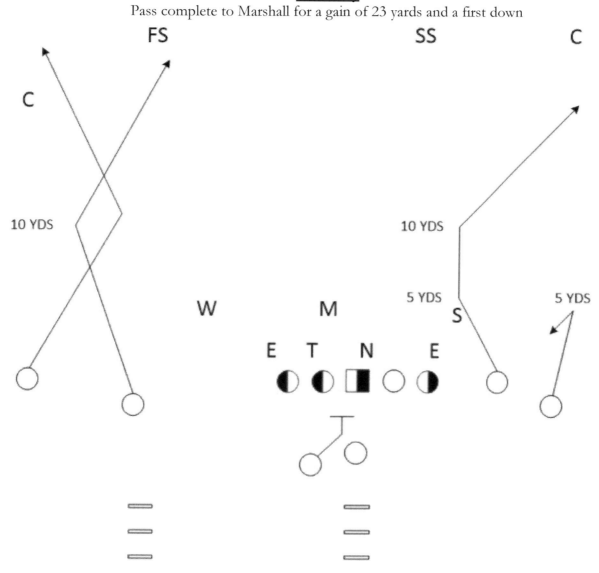

Analysis

Against this kind of end of game prevent defense, there's going to be this space open over the middle of the field. The defense does exactly what it's supposed to do, which is force a completion over the middle and in bounds. Interesting that the routes on the wide side of the field switch places not once but twice.

Oregon Drive 14 / Play 2 / 1ˢᵗ & 10 / -43 Yard Line / Right Hash / 0:17 4Q
Oregon 20 – OSU 42
Summary
Incomplete Pass

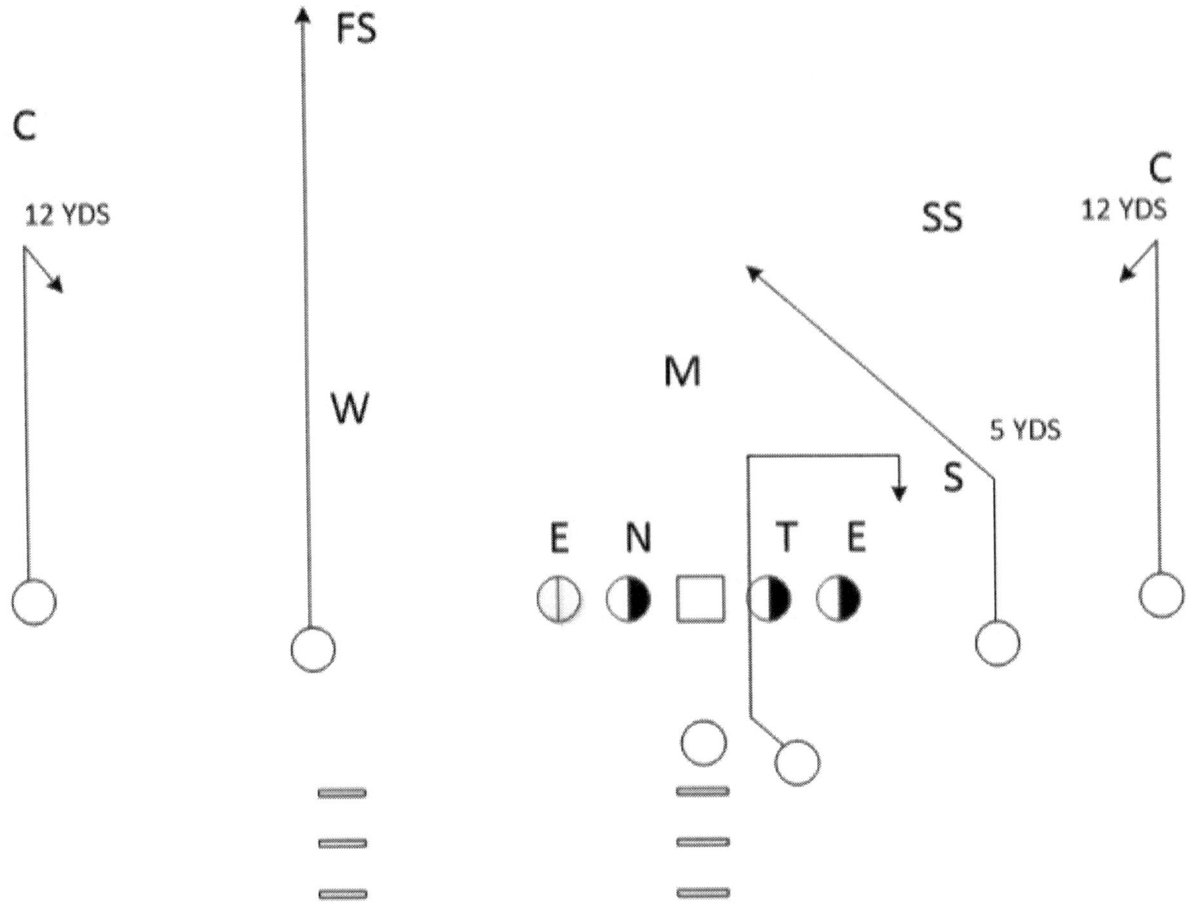

FS

C

12 YDS

SS

C

12 YDS

W

M

5 YDS

S

E   N   T   E

Analysis

Pre-snap, Mariota knows he's gonna be going to the wide side of the field because of the 4 on 3 to the boundary, as well as the huge cushion that corner is giving the X receiver. Unfortunately for Oregon, he short arms the throw and it's incomplete.

<u>Oregon Drive 14 / Play 3 / 2nd & 10 / -43 Yard Line / Right Hash / 0:08 4Q</u>
Oregon 20 – OSU 42
<u>Summary</u>
Interception! Pass intercepted by Eli Apple and returned for a gain of 8 yards

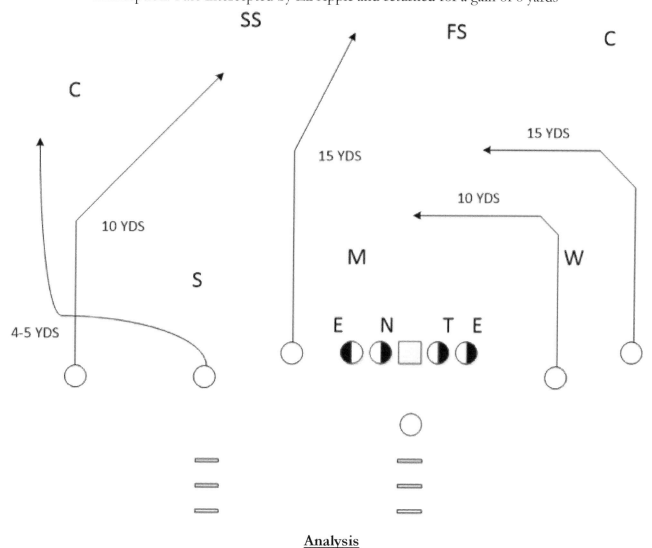

<u>Analysis</u>

This play is a bit of a long shot, not just because of the situation in the game, but also because it's an empty formation, which means it's a five-man protection scheme, and the offense is running all five guys down the field and attacking deep.

The pass rush forces Mariota out of the pocket, and his final pass as an Oregon Duck is intercepted.

Oregon Drive #14 Review

Oregon finds interesting ways to move the ball down the field. Hail Mary at the end of the game with Mariota throwing up a prayer, and Ohio State comes down with an interception to seal it.

ABOUT THE AUTHOR

Alex Kirby is a former high school and college football assistant who now writes about the game he loves at ProFootballStrategy.com and LifeAfterFootballBlog.com. He lives and works in Indianapolis, Indiana.

Made in the USA
Middletown, DE
26 April 2017